AI AND YOU

A Practical Guide to the
Age of Artificial Intelligence

Ravindra Dastikop

CONTENTS

PREFACE

The 21st century has been defined by rapid advancements in technology, with Artificial Intelligence (AI) emerging as one of the most transformative forces of our time. From revolutionizing industries to simplifying everyday tasks, AI is reshaping the way we live, work, and interact with the world around us. This book, *AI and You: A Practical Guide to the Age of Artificial Intelligence*, is an attempt to bridge the gap between AI's complexity and its practical implications for our lives.

The Importance of AI in Our Lives

AI is no longer a distant concept confined to research labs or sci-fi narratives. It is now deeply embedded in our lives—enhancing our smartphones, powering our virtual assistants, improving medical diagnoses, and even helping us combat global challenges like climate change. The rapid proliferation of AI-driven technologies has created a pressing need for understanding its mechanisms, opportunities, and ethical considerations.

This book aims to demystify AI for everyone, regardless of technical expertise, so that readers can navigate this technological revolution with confidence, curiosity, and responsibility.

Scope of the Book

This book offers a comprehensive overview of AI's applications, challenges, and future possibilities. It covers a wide range of topics, from AI's impact on education, healthcare, and creativity to its ethical dilemmas and societal implications. By addressing AI's role in both personal and professional spheres, the book seeks to empower readers to harness its potential effectively and responsibly.

Whether you're a student curious about AI, a professional seeking to integrate AI into your work, or simply a citizen of the world trying to keep pace with technology, this book provides insights tailored to your needs.

Structure of the Book

The book is organized into 20 chapters, each addressing a unique aspect of AI:

1. The first few chapters lay the foundation, introducing readers to AI's basics and its transformative impact on our everyday lives.
2. Subsequent chapters delve into AI's applications in specific domains such as education, healthcare, sustainability, and entertainment.
3. A significant portion of the book is devoted to ethical considerations, societal challenges, and the importance of responsible innovation.
4. The final chapters explore the future of AI, addressing emerging trends, potential risks, and the evolving relationship between humans and machines.

Each chapter includes:

- **Learning Objectives** to set the stage for what readers can expect.
- **Real-Life Examples** to illustrate AI's applications.
- **Quick Assessment Quizzes** to reinforce understanding.
- **Chapter Summaries and Points to Ponder** to encourage critical thinking.
- **References** for further exploration.

Key Features

1. **Comprehensive Yet Accessible**: The book balances technical depth with clarity, making it suitable for readers of varying expertise levels.

2. **Practical Focus**: Real-world applications and case studies help bridge the gap between theory and practice.
3. **Interactive Elements**: Quizzes and reflective prompts engage readers actively, enhancing retention and understanding.
4. **Global and Inclusive Perspective**: The book highlights AI's impact across diverse sectors and communities, emphasizing its potential to create a more equitable world.
5. **Forward-Looking Approach**: By addressing emerging trends and challenges, the book prepares readers for AI's future trajectory.

A Call to Action

As AI continues to evolve, so must our understanding and engagement with it. This book is not merely an introduction to AI but a call to action—urging readers to embrace its possibilities, navigate its challenges, and contribute to shaping a future where technology serves humanity's highest ideals.

I invite you to join me on this journey of discovery and reflection, as we explore how AI can empower us, challenge us, and ultimately redefine what it means to be human in an age of intelligence.

INTRODUCTION TO THE BOOK

Introduction

Artificial Intelligence (AI) is no longer a distant dream confined to science fiction; it is a transformative force that is reshaping every aspect of our lives. From the apps on your smartphone to global efforts addressing climate change, AI is an indispensable part of the modern world. But what exactly is AI? How does it work? And how can you, as an individual, harness its potential while navigating its complexities?

This book, *AI and You: A Practical Guide to the Age of Artificial Intelligence*, is designed to bridge the gap between curiosity and understanding. Whether you're an entrepreneur, student, professional, or someone simply intrigued by the rise of AI, this book offers insights, tools, and actionable strategies to thrive in the AI-driven era.

Learning Objectives for the Book

As you journey through this book, you will:

1. Understand what AI is, how it works, and its key applications.
2. Explore real-world examples of AI in diverse industries.
3. Gain insights into the ethical, social, and cultural implications of AI.
4. Learn practical ways to integrate AI tools into your personal and professional life.
5. Prepare for emerging trends and challenges in an AI-powered future.

Structure of the Book

This book is divided into 20 chapters, each focusing on a specific aspect of AI. It begins with foundational concepts and gradually explores advanced topics, real-world applications, and the future of AI. Each chapter is designed to offer:

1. **Clear Explanations:** Breaking down complex ideas into simple terms.
2. **Case Studies:** Global and regional examples, including specific examples from India.
3. **Practical Exercises:** Opportunities to explore AI tools and apply what you've learned.
4. **Ethical Discussions:** Addressing challenges and responsibilities in the AI landscape.
5. **Reflection and Engagement:** Questions and activities to deepen your understanding.

Why This Book?

AI is often portrayed as a mysterious, intimidating field reserved for tech experts. This book aims to dispel that myth. AI is for everyone, and understanding its potential can empower you to adapt, innovate, and contribute meaningfully to an AI-driven world.

Key Features

1. **Inclusive Perspective:** Designed for readers from all walks of life—no technical background required.
2. **Hands-On Approach:** Step-by-step guidance to explore popular AI tools and technologies.
3. **Balanced Insights:** Covering both opportunities and challenges, from groundbreaking innovations to ethical dilemmas.
4. **Cultural Relevance:** Examples tailored to diverse contexts, including India's AI advancements.

What You'll Gain

By the end of this book, you will have:

- A clear understanding of AI fundamentals.
- Knowledge of how AI is shaping industries like healthcare, education, and finance.

- Insights into how to use AI responsibly and ethically.
- A roadmap for leveraging AI in your personal and professional journey.

Reflection Questions

1. What comes to mind when you hear the term "Artificial Intelligence"?
2. How has AI already influenced your daily life, directly or indirectly?
3. What are your greatest hopes—and fears—about AI's role in the future?

Points to Ponder

- AI is a tool, not a replacement. How can it complement human creativity and problem-solving?
- In an era driven by AI, what skills or values should we nurture to maintain our humanity?

Preview of Chapter 1: Introduction to AI – Understanding the Basics

The first chapter will lay the groundwork by exploring what AI is, its key components, and how it has evolved over time. You will learn about the various types of AI, its core technologies, and the ethical considerations surrounding its use.

Prepare to dive into the fascinating world of Artificial Intelligence and discover how it can shape your future!

CHAPTER 1

Understanding the Basics

Learning Objectives

By the end of this chapter, you will be able to:

1. Define Artificial Intelligence (AI) and explain its importance.
2. Distinguish between Narrow AI, General AI, and Superintelligent AI.
3. Understand key concepts like Machine Learning, Neural Networks, and Natural Language Processing.
4. Recognize the historical evolution of AI and its current impact on society.

1.1 What is AI?

Artificial Intelligence (AI) refers to the simulation of human intelligence in machines that are programmed to think, learn, and make decisions. AI encompasses various technologies that enable machines to mimic cognitive functions such as problem-solving, understanding language, and recognizing patterns.

Key Features of AI:

- Learning from experience (Machine Learning).
- Reasoning and decision-making.
- Adapting to new inputs and environments.

Real-Life Examples:

- Virtual assistants like Siri and Alexa.
- Recommendation systems on Netflix and Amazon.
- Autonomous vehicles like Tesla's self-driving cars.

Quick Assessment Quiz

1. Define Artificial Intelligence in your own words.

2. List three examples of AI you encounter in daily life.

1.2 Types of AI

AI can be classified into three types based on capabilities:

1. **Narrow AI:** AI systems specialized in one task, e.g., Google Translate.
2. **General AI:** Hypothetical AI that can perform any intellectual task a human can do.
3. **Superintelligent AI:** A futuristic concept where AI surpasses human intelligence in all domains.

Comparison Table

Type	Definition	Examples
Narrow AI	Performs specific tasks.	ChatGPT, Spotify.
General AI	Matches human cognitive abilities.	Still theoretical.
Superintelligent AI	Surpasses human intelligence.	AI in sci-fi movies.

Quick Assessment Quiz

1. Explain the difference between Narrow AI and General AI.
2. Provide an example of Narrow AI you've used recently.

1.3 Key AI Technologies

AI comprises various technologies working together:

1. **Machine Learning (ML):** Enables systems to learn from data. Examples: Fraud detection in banking.

2. **Neural Networks:** Mimics the human brain to recognize patterns. Examples: Image recognition in Facebook.
3. **Natural Language Processing (NLP):** Helps machines understand and respond to human language. Examples: ChatGPT, Google Assistant.

Case Study: AI in Indian Agriculture
AI is transforming agriculture in India. Tools like Microsoft's AI Sowing App provide farmers with timely advice, improving crop yield and sustainability.

Quick Assessment Quiz

1. What is the primary goal of Machine Learning?
2. Name an Indian AI application in agriculture.

1.4 The Evolution of AI

AI has evolved significantly since its inception:

1. **1940s-1950s:** Foundations laid with the development of computers.
2. **1960s-1970s:** AI programs focused on problem-solving and games like chess.
3. **1980s-1990s:** Machine Learning gained prominence.
4. **2000s-Today:** Explosion of AI applications in diverse fields like healthcare and finance.

Milestone Example:

In 1997, IBM's Deep Blue defeated world chess champion Garry Kasparov, showcasing AI's potential.

Quick Assessment Quiz

1. Mention one key milestone in AI history.
2. How has AI changed in the past decade?

Chapter Summary

- **Definition:** AI mimics human intelligence in machines.
- **Types of AI:** Narrow AI is prevalent today; General AI and Superintelligent AI remain conceptual.
- **Key Technologies:** Machine Learning, Neural Networks, and NLP drive modern AI systems.
- **Evolution:** AI has progressed from basic programs to advanced systems influencing daily life.

Points to Ponder

1. Why is it important to understand the basics of AI?
2. What role does AI play in shaping the future of society?
3. How can individuals prepare for an AI-driven world?

Preview of Chapter 2: AI in Everyday Life – How It's Transforming Our World

Chapter 2 will delve into the practical applications of AI that impact our daily routines. From personalized recommendations to smart home devices, you'll explore how AI makes life more convenient and efficient.

References

1. Russell, S., & Norvig, P. (2020). *Artificial Intelligence: A Modern Approach.* Purchase Here
2. Microsoft AI India. *Empowering Agriculture with AI.* Read More
3. Marr, B. (2021). *What is Artificial Intelligence?* Forbes. Read Here

CHAPTER 2

AI in Everyday Life – How It's Transforming Our World

Recap of Chapter 1

In Chapter 1, we laid the foundation by exploring what Artificial Intelligence (AI) is, its history, types, and key technologies. We discussed how AI has evolved from an experimental idea into a transformative force shaping our daily lives. With this understanding, let's now dive into how AI is seamlessly integrated into the fabric of our everyday experiences.

Learning Objectives

By the end of this chapter, readers will:

1. Recognize the applications of AI in routine tasks.
2. Understand the impact of AI on consumer services like entertainment, healthcare, and shopping.
3. Explore Indian and global examples of AI-driven innovation in daily life.
4. Evaluate the benefits and limitations of AI in everyday use.

Section 1: AI in Personal Devices

AI is embedded in the personal devices we use daily, enhancing convenience and functionality.

- **Smart Assistants:** Tools like Siri, Alexa, and Google Assistant help with reminders, searches, and home automation.
- **AI in Smartphones:** Features such as facial recognition, predictive text, and camera optimizations rely on AI.

Quick Assessment Quiz

1. Name two ways AI improves smartphone usability.
2. Which smart assistant do you use most often, and why?

Section 2: AI in Entertainment

AI curates our entertainment experiences by personalizing content and enhancing creativity.

- **Content Recommendations:** Platforms like Netflix, YouTube, and Spotify use algorithms to suggest shows, videos, and music.
- **Gaming AI:**
  Games like *Chess.com* and *FIFA* integrate AI for challenging opponents and immersive environments.
- **Indian Context:** Hotstar's recommendation engine powered by AI algorithms.

Quick Assessment Quiz

1. How does Netflix use AI to personalize your viewing experience?
2. What role does AI play in gaming platforms?

Section 3: AI in Healthcare at Home

AI empowers individuals to monitor health and wellness more effectively.

- **Wearable Devices:** Smartwatches and fitness trackers like Fitbit analyze health data such as heart rate and sleep patterns.
- **Telemedicine Platforms:** AI-powered apps like Practo and 1mg in India connect users with doctors and provide health solutions.

Quick Assessment Quiz

1. List two wearable devices that use AI to track health data.

2. How has AI impacted telemedicine services in India?

Section 4: AI in Shopping and E-commerce

AI is redefining how consumers shop online and offline.

- **Personalized Shopping Experience:** Platforms like Amazon and Flipkart use AI to recommend products based on user preferences.
- **Customer Support Chatbots:** AI chatbots handle queries and provide seamless support.
- **Visual Search Tools:** Tools like Pinterest Lens allow users to search for products using images.

Indian Case Study: Flipkart's AI-driven logistics for faster delivery.

Quick Assessment Quiz

1. Describe one AI feature used by e-commerce platforms.
2. Give an example of AI-powered visual search in e-commerce.

Section 5: Challenges and Limitations

While AI enhances convenience, it also raises concerns:

- **Privacy Issues:** Data collection and surveillance risks.
- **Digital Divide:** Not everyone has access to AI-powered tools.
- **Bias in Algorithms:** AI recommendations may reflect biases.

Quick Assessment Quiz

1. Name one privacy concern associated with AI in everyday use.
2. How can AI contribute to the digital divide?

Chapter Summary

- AI seamlessly integrates into personal devices, entertainment, healthcare, and shopping.
- Indian platforms like Hotstar, Flipkart, and Practo showcase localized AI innovation.
- Challenges such as privacy and bias must be addressed to ensure equitable AI use.

Points to Ponder

1. In what ways has AI improved your daily experiences?

2. How can governments and organizations address the challenges of AI accessibility?

3. What steps can users take to safeguard their privacy while using AI-powered tools?

Preview of Chapter 3: The Role of AI in the Workplace – Opportunities and Challenges

The next chapter will explore how AI is transforming the workplace, from automating tasks to driving innovation. We'll discuss its implications for different industries, skills in demand, and ethical challenges.

References

1. "How AI Helps Netflix Personalize Your Experience" – Netflix Tech Blog
2. "AI in Healthcare in India: An Overview" – NITI Aayog Report
3. "How Flipkart Uses AI for Customer-Centric Solutions" – Flipkart Stories

CHAPTER 3

The Role of AI in the Workplace – Opportunities and Challenges

Learning Objectives

By the end of this chapter, readers will:

1. Understand how AI is transforming various industries.
2. Identify key AI tools and technologies used in workplaces.
3. Recognize challenges posed by AI adoption and strategies to address them.
4. Explore real-world examples of AI applications in workplaces, including in India.

Recap of Chapter 2: AI in Everyday Life

In the previous chapter, we explored how AI is integrated into our daily lives through tools like virtual assistants, recommendation systems, and navigation apps. We examined global and Indian case studies, emphasizing AI's role in enhancing convenience and productivity.

Content Overview

Section 1: How AI is Transforming the Workplace

AI is revolutionizing industries by automating repetitive tasks, enhancing decision-making, and fostering innovation. Key areas include:

- **Automation of Routine Tasks:** AI tools streamline workflows, reduce errors, and save time.
- **Enhanced Decision-Making:** AI-powered analytics provide insights for strategic planning.
- **Talent Acquisition:** Tools like LinkedIn Recruiter AI simplify hiring by identifying the best candidates.

Case Study:

In India, Tata Consultancy Services (TCS) uses AI-based platforms to enhance employee productivity and automate business processes.

Quick Assessment Quiz:

1. Name two ways AI enhances decision-making in workplaces.
2. Give an example of an AI tool used for talent acquisition.

Section 2: Popular AI Tools in Workplaces

AI is embedded in various workplace tools, such as:

1. **CRM and Sales:** Salesforce Einstein uses AI to predict customer behavior.
- Explore Salesforce Einstein
2. **Customer Support:** ChatGPT and Zendesk provide AI-driven customer service solutions.
- Discover Zendesk AI
3. **HR Management:** Tools like Zoho Recruit help streamline recruitment processes.
- Learn about Zoho Recruit
4. **Marketing Automation:** HubSpot and Mailchimp use AI for targeted marketing.

Quick Assessment Quiz:

5. Which AI tool is used for customer relationship management?
6. Name an AI-powered marketing automation platform.

Section 3: Challenges of AI Adoption in Workplaces

While AI offers numerous benefits, challenges include:

- **Resistance to Change:** Employees fear job displacement due to automation.
- **Bias in AI Systems:** Unfair decisions due to biased training data.
- **Integration Costs:** High initial investments for AI infrastructure.

Strategies to Overcome Challenges:

- Upskilling employees in AI technologies.
- Regularly auditing AI systems to minimize bias.
- Exploring affordable AI solutions like cloud-based platforms.

Case Study:

Wipro's AI program in India emphasizes reskilling its workforce to adapt to AI-driven changes.

Quick Assessment Quiz:

1. What is a common concern employees have about AI?
2. Suggest one strategy to address AI bias.

Chapter Summary

- **AI's Role in Workplaces:** From automation to decision-making, AI is transforming how we work.
- **AI Tools:** Popular tools include Salesforce Einstein, Zoho Recruit, and HubSpot.
- **Challenges:** Resistance to change, bias, and integration costs remain barriers to AI adoption.
- **Solutions:** Upskilling employees and using ethical AI practices are crucial.

Points to Ponder

- How can businesses strike a balance between automation and preserving jobs?

- What role should governments play in regulating AI in workplaces?

Preview of Chapter 4: AI and Creativity – Partnering with Machines for Innovation

The next chapter explores AI's role in creative fields like art, music, and storytelling. Discover how AI is empowering creators while redefining creativity.

References

1. "Salesforce Einstein Overview." Salesforce. Explore Here
2. "AI-Powered Customer Service by Zendesk." Zendesk. Read More
3. "Recruitment Simplified with Zoho Recruit." Zoho. Learn More
4. "AI in Wipro." Wipro Official Site. Explore AI Solutions

Chapter 4
AI and Creativity – Partnering with Machines for Innovation

Learning Objectives

By the end of this chapter, readers will:

1. Understand how AI is used in creative fields such as art, music, and writing.
2. Explore specific tools and platforms for creative collaboration with AI.
3. Gain insights into how human creativity and AI can coexist and enhance one another.
4. Analyze real-world case studies, including examples from India.
5. Reflect on the ethical and cultural implications of AI in creative processes.

Introduction

Creativity has long been considered a uniquely human trait, a realm where emotions, imagination, and innovation converge. However, with the advent of Artificial Intelligence, this perception is changing. AI is now playing a vital role in creative fields, from generating art to composing music, writing novels, and designing products. This chapter explores how humans and machines collaborate in the creative process and examines tools and case studies that demonstrate this exciting synergy.

1. AI in Visual Art

How AI Generates Art

AI tools like neural networks use vast datasets to create unique and innovative pieces of art. Generative Adversarial Networks (GANs) play a significant role, with algorithms capable of producing anything from realistic portraits to abstract visuals.

Case Study: Indian Artists Adopting AI Art

Indian digital artists like Harshit Agrawal are pushing boundaries by using AI to create unique art pieces that blend technology with traditional aesthetics.

Quick Assessment Quiz

- Q1: What are GANs, and how do they contribute to AI art?
- Q2: Name one Indian artist leveraging AI for creative purposes.

Tool Recommendations

- **DALL·E**: A tool for creating highly detailed images based on text prompts. Explore DALL·E
- **DeepArt.io**: A platform that transforms photos into artwork. Try DeepArt.io

2. AI in Music Composition

How AI Composes Music

AI algorithms analyze music theory, genres, and patterns to compose original pieces. Tools like OpenAI's MuseNet can mimic famous composers or produce entirely new melodies.

Case Study: Indian Music Platforms Using AI

Indian startups like Flutin and Beatoven.ai use AI to help musicians create soundtracks and personalized playlists efficiently.

Quick Assessment Quiz

- Q1: How does MuseNet assist in music composition?
- Q2: Mention an Indian platform that integrates AI for music creation.

- *Tool Recommendations*
- **MuseNet**:
  AI-generated music compositions. Explore MuseNet
- **AIVA (Artificial Intelligence Virtual Artist)**:
  Create music for film, games, and commercials. Try
  AIVA

3. AI in Writing and Storytelling

Enhancing Content Creation

AI writing tools analyze language patterns and user input to generate stories, articles, or poetry. These tools save time while opening new avenues for creative storytelling.

Case Study: AI in Indian Media

Indian media outlets like The Times of India use AI for content generation, including personalized news summaries.

Quick Assessment Quiz

- Q1: How do AI tools assist in storytelling?
- Q2: Name an Indian media organization that uses AI for content.

Tool Recommendations

- **ChatGPT**: A conversational AI tool for writing assistance. Use ChatGPT
- **Writesonic**: AI-driven content creation platform. Try Writesonic

4. AI in Product Design and Architecture

Revolutionizing Design Processes

AI accelerates the design process by analyzing user preferences, testing prototypes, and suggesting improvements. Architects and product designers use AI to enhance functionality and aesthetics.

Case Study: Indian Firms Embracing AI in Design

Companies like Tata Elxsi are integrating AI to streamline industrial and product design processes.

Quick Assessment Quiz

- Q1: How does AI optimize design workflows?
- Q2: Provide an example of an Indian firm using AI in design.

Tool Recommendations

- **Runway ML**: A tool for creative professionals integrating AI into design. Explore Runway ML
- **Figma with Plugins**: Collaborative design with AI-powered tools. Try Figma

Ethical and Cultural Implications

Balancing AI with Human Creativity

While AI can assist and inspire, it raises questions about originality, intellectual property, and cultural authenticity. This section examines the importance of maintaining human oversight in creative processes.

Quick Assessment Quiz

- Q1: What ethical concerns arise in AI-driven creativity?
- Q2: How can AI complement rather than replace human creativity?

Chapter Summary

- AI is revolutionizing creative fields, including art, music, writing, and design.
- Tools like DALL·E, MuseNet, and Runway ML empower creators with innovative capabilities.

- Indian artists, musicians, and companies are leveraging AI for unique cultural and commercial projects.
- Ethical considerations must guide the integration of AI into creative practices.

Points to Ponder

1. Can an AI-generated painting be considered "art"? Why or why not?
2. How can traditional artists and writers collaborate with AI to enhance their work?
3. What safeguards should be in place to ensure AI respects cultural nuances?

Preview of Chapter 5: Harnessing AI for Personal Growth and Learning

The next chapter will explore how AI tools can aid in self-improvement, productivity, and skill-building. From AI-powered language tutors to task management systems, discover how technology can empower your personal development journey.

References

1. "The Art of AI – Transforming Creativity" – DeepArt.io
2. "AI in Music Composition: MuseNet" – MuseNet
3. "AI in Media – Indian Perspectives" – The Times of India
4. "Runway ML: A Creative AI Toolkit" – Runway ML
5. "Beatoven.ai: AI for Indian Music Creators" – Beatoven.ai

CHAPTER 5

Harnessing AI for Personal Growth and Learning

Learning Objectives

By the end of this chapter, you will:

1. Understand how AI enhances personalized learning experiences.
2. Identify AI-powered tools and platforms for skill-building and productivity.
3. Explore case studies and real-life examples, particularly in the Indian context.
4. Recognize ethical challenges in using AI for self-improvement and strategies to overcome them.

Introduction

The rapid advancement of AI has made it a critical tool for personal development and lifelong learning. Whether you are mastering a new skill, pursuing academic goals, or boosting productivity, AI is transforming traditional approaches. This chapter offers a deep dive into the diverse applications of AI in personal growth, from tailored education to intelligent productivity tools.

Section 1: AI in Personalized Learning

What is Personalized Learning?

Personalized learning tailors educational experiences to the unique needs, abilities, and pace of each individual. Unlike traditional methods, AI leverages data to create custom learning paths that maximize efficiency and engagement.

Key Examples of AI in Personalized Learning

1. **Duolingo**: This language-learning app uses AI algorithms to adjust lessons based on the learner's strengths and weaknesses, ensuring gradual and effective progress.
- Website: Duolingo
2. **Khan Academy (Khanmigo)**: AI provides detailed feedback and custom recommendations for subjects such as math and science.
- Website: Khan Academy
3. **BYJU'S**: As one of India's leading ed-tech platforms, BYJU'S uses AI to personalize lessons and offer performance-based insights.
- Website: BYJU'S

Additional Insights

AI in education isn't limited to platforms; it also involves smart classrooms and gamified experiences to make learning interactive and fun.

Quick Assessment Quiz

4. What makes personalized learning unique compared to traditional learning methods?
5. Provide two examples of AI platforms that support personalized education.
6. How does BYJU'S leverage AI in India to enhance learning?

Section 2: AI for Skill Development

AI Tools for Upskilling

1. **LinkedIn Learning**: Personalized course recommendations based on user goals and professional trends.
- Website: LinkedIn Learning

2. **Coursera**: Uses AI to suggest courses and create custom learning schedules.
- Website: Coursera
3. **Relevel by Unacademy**: Focuses on industry-relevant courses in India, helping individuals prepare for competitive job markets.
- Website: Relevel

Indian Case Study: Skill India Mission

Under the Skill India Mission, AI tools are being integrated into training programs to bridge skill gaps in sectors like manufacturing, IT, and agriculture. AI provides real-time analytics and performance feedback to optimize the learning experience.

Additional Examples

- **TCS iON**: AI-driven upskilling solutions in India.
- **AICTE's NEAT Initiative**: AI-powered tools for engineering students.

Quick Assessment Quiz

4. What are the advantages of AI-driven upskilling platforms like LinkedIn Learning?
5. Discuss an Indian initiative that uses AI to enhance skill-building programs.

Section 3: AI as a Personal Productivity Assistant

How AI Improves Productivity

AI tools streamline workflows, enhance decision-making, and automate repetitive tasks. These systems are especially valuable in managing time, prioritizing tasks, and organizing information.

Popular AI Productivity Tools

1. **Notion AI**: Combines task management with AI-generated insights, allowing users to organize information and brainstorm ideas effectively.

- Website: Notion AI

2. **Grammarly**: Automatically improves writing by suggesting corrections for grammar, tone, and clarity.

- Website: Grammarly

3. **Google Assistant**: A smart assistant that handles scheduling, reminders, and searches, offering seamless integration with daily life.

- Website: Google Assistant

Case Study: Productivity Boost with AI

A freelance writer used Grammarly and Notion AI to enhance content quality and streamline idea generation, resulting in increased productivity and client satisfaction.

Quick Assessment Quiz

1. List three AI tools that enhance personal productivity and their features.
2. Explain how Google Assistant can help organize your day.

Section 4: Ethical Considerations of AI in Personal Growth

Key Challenges

1. **Privacy Concerns**: AI platforms often require access to sensitive personal data.
2. **Over-Reliance on AI**: Excessive dependence on AI might impair problem-solving and creativity.

Strategies to Overcome Challenges

- Opt for platforms that emphasize data privacy and security.
- Balance AI usage with traditional methods to retain critical thinking skills.

Indian Context

Indian AI-powered platforms, such as DigiLocker, focus on secure digital interactions while emphasizing privacy.

Quick Assessment Quiz

1. Why is data privacy a critical concern for AI platforms?
2. What steps can you take to avoid over-reliance on AI?

Chapter Summary

This chapter explored the transformative potential of AI in personal growth and learning. Key highlights include:

- AI empowers personalized learning through adaptive tools like Duolingo and BYJU'S.
- Platforms like LinkedIn Learning and Relevel enhance skill development.
- Productivity tools such as Grammarly and Notion AI streamline daily tasks.
- Ethical challenges, such as data privacy and over-reliance, require thoughtful strategies.

Points to Ponder

1. How has AI influenced your learning and productivity habits?
2. What steps can you take to use AI tools responsibly?
3. Can AI fully replace traditional methods of learning and self-improvement? Why or why not?

Preview of Chapter 6: Ethics and Responsibility in AI: Navigating the Challenges

In **Chapter 6**, we will dive into the ethical challenges of AI, including issues of bias, transparency, and accountability. The chapter will provide actionable strategies to navigate these challenges while harnessing AI's potential responsibly.

References

1. **Duolingo** - Duolingo Website
2. **Khan Academy** - Khan Academy Website
3. **BYJU'S** - BYJU'S Website
4. **LinkedIn Learning** - LinkedIn Learning Website
5. **Coursera** - Coursera Website
6. **Grammarly** - Grammarly Website
7. **Skill India Mission** - Skill India Mission Website
8. **Notion AI** - Notion AI Website

Chapter Review Quiz

1. Define personalized learning and name two AI tools that support it.
2. Discuss the role of AI in upskilling. Provide an example of an Indian initiative.
3. What are the ethical challenges of using AI for personal growth, and how can they be addressed?
4. Name two AI tools for productivity and explain how they can simplify your tasks.

CHAPTER 6

Ethics and Responsibility in AI: Navigating the Challenges

Learning Objectives

By the end of this chapter, you will:

1. Understand the key ethical concerns surrounding AI, including bias, transparency, and accountability.
2. Learn how organizations and governments address these challenges.
3. Explore strategies to promote responsible AI use in personal and professional settings.
4. Examine real-world examples of ethical dilemmas and solutions in AI implementation.

Recap of Previous Chapter

In Chapter 5, we explored how AI tools can revolutionize personal growth and learning. We discussed personalized learning, AI-powered skill development, productivity tools, and ethical considerations in using AI responsibly.

Section 1: Key Ethical Concerns in AI

1.1 Bias in AI Systems

AI systems can reflect and amplify biases present in the data they are trained on. This can lead to discrimination in areas like hiring, lending, and law enforcement.

Example:

- In the U.S., a hiring AI tool showed bias against women by favoring male applicants due to historical data biases.

Indian Example:

- Some AI-powered government services faced challenges with regional language dialects, leading to accessibility issues for non-English speakers.

1.2 Lack of Transparency

AI systems often function as "black boxes," making it difficult to understand how decisions are made. This lack of transparency can erode trust and accountability.

Example:

- An AI-driven credit scoring system in India lacked clarity in explaining low credit scores, causing frustration among users.

1.3 Accountability and Responsibility

Who is responsible when AI systems fail? This question is central to ethical AI use, particularly in high-stakes areas like healthcare and autonomous vehicles.

Quick Assessment Quiz

1. Define bias in AI systems and provide one real-world example.
2. Why is transparency critical in AI systems?
3. Discuss the challenges of assigning accountability in AI failures.

Section 2: Addressing Ethical Challenges in AI

2.1 Strategies for Reducing Bias

- **Diverse Data Sets**: Use data sets that are representative of different demographics and contexts.
- **Regular Audits**: Conduct ongoing evaluations of AI systems to identify and address bias.

Case Study:

- A major ed-tech company in India revamped its AI models by incorporating data from underrepresented regions, improving inclusivity and accuracy.

2.2 Improving Transparency

- **Explainable AI**: Developing models that provide clear explanations for their decisions.
- **Regulations**: Governments worldwide, including India, are pushing for AI transparency through data privacy laws like the **Digital Personal Data Protection Act 2023**.

Example:

- The Reserve Bank of India (RBI) introduced guidelines for AI in banking to ensure decision-making processes are auditable and transparent.

2.3 Enhancing Accountability

- Define clear roles for AI developers, deployers, and users.
- Create legal frameworks for liability in AI-related failures.

Quick Assessment Quiz

1. What is explainable AI, and how can it enhance trust?
2. Name an Indian law aimed at improving AI transparency and explain its significance.
3. List two strategies to reduce bias in AI systems.

Section 3: Promoting Responsible AI Use

3.1 Ethical AI Principles

- **Fairness**: Ensure AI systems treat all individuals equitably.

- **Privacy**: Safeguard user data with robust security measures.
- **Inclusivity**: Design AI systems that accommodate diverse user needs.

3.2 The Role of Organizations

- **Tech Companies**: Implement internal ethics boards and guidelines.
- **Educational Institutions**: Include AI ethics in curricula to build awareness among future developers.

Example:

- Indian IT giants like TCS and Infosys have established AI ethics frameworks to guide their innovations responsibly.

Government and Global Efforts

- **NITI Aayog's AI Policy**: India's approach to ethical AI emphasizes inclusivity and transparency.
- **UNESCO AI Ethics Framework**: Provides global guidelines to balance AI's benefits and risks.

Quick Assessment Quiz

1. What are three ethical principles for responsible AI use?
2. How are Indian organizations promoting AI ethics?
3. Name an international framework for AI ethics and its purpose.

Chapter Summary

This chapter addressed the critical ethical challenges of AI, including bias, transparency, and accountability. Strategies to overcome these challenges, such as using diverse data sets, explainable AI, and clear legal frameworks, were explored. The chapter also highlighted the importance of ethical principles and collaborative efforts by organizations and governments to promote responsible AI use.

Points to Ponder

1. How can bias in AI systems be minimized without compromising efficiency?
2. Why is explainability crucial for building trust in AI?
3. What roles do individuals and institutions play in fostering ethical AI practices?

Preview of Chapter 7: AI and Society: Balancing Progress and Privacy

In **Chapter 7**, we will explore the societal implications of AI, focusing on the delicate balance between technological progress and privacy concerns. Key topics include data ownership, surveillance ethics, and AI's impact on social structures.

References

1. NITI Aayog AI Policy - NITI Aayog Website
2. Digital Personal Data Protection Act 2023 - Official Gazette
3. UNESCO AI Ethics Framework - UNESCO Website
4. Infosys AI Ethics Framework - Infosys Website
5. Reserve Bank of India AI Guidelines - RBI Website
6. Explainable AI by IBM - IBM AI Explainability 360

Chapter Review Quiz

1. What are the three main ethical challenges in AI?
2. Provide examples of strategies to reduce AI bias.
3. Explain the significance of transparency in AI systems.
4. Discuss the role of organizations in promoting ethical AI practices.

CHAPTER 7

AI and Society: Balancing Progress and Privacy

Learning Objectives

By the end of this chapter, you will:

1. Understand how AI impacts societal structures and daily life.
2. Analyze the balance between AI-driven progress and privacy protection.
3. Explore the ethical dilemmas posed by surveillance and data collection.
4. Examine global and local regulations addressing AI-related societal concerns.
5. Learn practical steps for individuals and organizations to safeguard privacy.

Recap of Previous Chapter

In Chapter 6, we explored the ethical challenges of AI, focusing on issues like bias, transparency, and accountability. We also discussed strategies for promoting responsible AI use, emphasizing fairness, inclusivity, and collaborative efforts by governments and organizations.

Section 1: AI's Impact on Society

1.1 Transforming Daily Life

AI influences everyday activities, from virtual assistants and recommendation algorithms to personalized healthcare and smart cities.

Example:

- **Global**: AI-driven navigation apps like Google Maps optimize travel routes using real-time data.

- **India**: The Aarogya Setu app, powered by AI, helped track and control the spread of COVID-19 during the pandemic.

1.2 Redefining Social Structures

AI reshapes employment, education, and communication, offering new opportunities while raising concerns about job displacement and inequality.

Case Study:

- India's **Skill India Mission** integrates AI to identify skill gaps and provide training for future-ready jobs.

Quick Assessment Quiz

1. Name two ways AI transforms daily life.
2. How has AI influenced India's workforce through initiatives like Skill India?
3. Discuss a potential downside of AI's impact on social structures.

Section 2: Privacy Concerns in the Age of AI

2.1 The Rise of Surveillance Systems

AI-powered surveillance raises privacy concerns, especially in areas like facial recognition and predictive policing.

Example:

- **Global**: China's widespread use of facial recognition technology for monitoring citizens.
- **India**: The Hyderabad Police's use of AI-based surveillance to enhance public safety, raising debates about data security.

2.2 Data Collection and Misuse

AI relies heavily on data, often collected without users' informed consent. This can lead to unauthorized data sharing or misuse.

Example:

- Social media platforms like Facebook faced scrutiny for mishandling user data during the Cambridge Analytica scandal.

2.3 Balancing Innovation and Privacy

Governments and organizations must strike a balance between harnessing AI's potential and safeguarding individual privacy rights.

Quick Assessment Quiz

1. Describe the role of AI in modern surveillance.
2. Provide an example of data misuse in an AI context.
3. Why is it challenging to balance AI-driven innovation with privacy protection?

Section 3: Safeguarding Privacy in an AI-Driven World

3.1 Personal Strategies for Privacy

- Use privacy-centric tools like VPNs and encrypted messaging apps.
- Regularly update privacy settings on social media and online services.

Example:

- Indian startups like **Kavach** develop secure communication tools for individuals and businesses.

Organizational Approaches

- Implement data minimization practices, collecting only necessary information.

- Train employees on ethical data handling and privacy laws.

Case Study:

- Infosys enhanced its AI systems by prioritizing data security measures to comply with global regulations.

3.3 Government and Policy Measures

- **India**: The **Digital Personal Data Protection Act 2023** focuses on protecting citizens' data privacy.
- **Global**: The **EU's General Data Protection Regulation (GDPR)** sets a benchmark for privacy laws.

Quick Assessment Quiz

1. List two personal strategies for safeguarding privacy.
2. What is data minimization, and why is it important?
3. Name two privacy regulations and explain their significance.

Chapter Summary

This chapter examined the societal implications of AI, highlighting its transformative impact on daily life and social structures. We explored privacy concerns related to surveillance and data collection and discussed strategies for individuals, organizations, and governments to balance AI-driven progress with privacy protection.

Points to Ponder

1. How can societies balance the benefits of AI with ethical concerns?
2. Are privacy laws keeping pace with the rapid advancements in AI?
3. What role should individuals play in ensuring their own data privacy?

Preview of Chapter 8: The Future of AI: Emerging Trends and Technologies

In **Chapter 8**, we will delve into emerging AI technologies, including quantum computing, generative AI, and robotics. We'll explore how these trends shape the future of industries and society while discussing their challenges and opportunities.

References

1. Aarogya Setu App - Aarogya Setu
2. Digital Personal Data Protection Act 2023 - Official Gazette
3. Skill India Mission - Skill India Portal
4. General Data Protection Regulation (GDPR) - EU GDPR
5. Infosys Privacy Policies - Infosys
6. Cambridge Analytica Scandal - BBC News

Chapter Review Quiz

1. Identify two societal changes AI has brought to daily life.
2. Discuss the ethical concerns of AI-powered surveillance.
3. Name two key regulations addressing AI-related privacy concerns.
4. Explain how individuals can protect their privacy in the age of AI.

CHAPTER 8

The Future of AI: Emerging Trends and Technologies

Learning Objectives

By the end of this chapter, you will:

1. Understand key emerging trends in AI, such as generative AI, quantum computing, and autonomous systems.
2. Analyze how these advancements will shape industries and society.
3. Explore the challenges and ethical dilemmas associated with new AI technologies.
4. Identify opportunities for individuals and organizations to leverage these trends effectively.

Recap of Previous Chapter

In Chapter 7, we examined AI's societal impact, focusing on its transformative effects on daily life and privacy concerns. We discussed strategies for safeguarding privacy and the role of governments, organizations, and individuals in navigating AI's ethical challenges.

Section 1: Emerging Trends in AI

1.1 Generative AI

Generative AI systems, such as OpenAI's ChatGPT and DALL·E, create new content, including text, images, and music, based on input data.

Applications:

- Content creation for media and marketing.
- Drug discovery through protein modeling (e.g., AlphaFold by DeepMind).
- Creative industries, including art and literature.

Indian Example:

- Startups like **Rephrase.ai** use generative AI to create personalized video content for businesses.

Challenges:

- Potential misuse for creating deepfakes and misinformation.
- Copyright and intellectual property concerns.

1.2 Quantum Computing and AI

Quantum computing has the potential to revolutionize AI by solving problems too complex for traditional computers.

Applications:

- Advanced optimization problems in logistics and finance.
- Faster and more accurate drug discovery.

Indian Example:

- The Indian government's **Quantum Mission** aims to advance quantum computing, fostering its integration with AI technologies.

Challenges:

- High costs and technical barriers to implementation.

1.3 Autonomous Systems

From self-driving cars to drones, autonomous systems are transforming industries like transportation, agriculture, and defense.

Applications:

- Self-driving vehicles improving road safety and reducing emissions.

- AI-powered drones optimizing crop monitoring in agriculture.

Indian Example:

- Companies like **Agnikul Cosmos** use AI to enhance autonomous satellite launch systems.

Quick Assessment Quiz

1. Define generative AI and list two of its applications.
2. What is the significance of quantum computing in AI?
3. Discuss a real-world application of autonomous systems in India.

Section 2: Societal and Industry Impacts of Emerging AI Technologies

2.1 Transforming Industries

- **Healthcare**: AI-driven diagnostic tools and personalized medicine.
- **Finance**: Fraud detection and algorithmic trading powered by advanced AI.
- **Education**: AI tutors delivering adaptive learning experiences.

Indian Example:

- AI-based telemedicine platforms like **Practo** enhance remote healthcare delivery in rural areas.

2.2 Enhancing Global Connectivity

AI innovations bridge the digital divide, enabling global access to education, healthcare, and information.

Case Study:

- The **AI4Bharat initiative** develops tools for language translation and natural language processing to make AI accessible in regional Indian languages.

- *Risks and Ethical Challenges*
- Job displacement due to automation in manufacturing and services.
- Increasing reliance on AI systems, leading to vulnerabilities in cybersecurity.
- Ethical concerns in the deployment of autonomous weapons.

Quick Assessment Quiz

1. Name two industries transformed by emerging AI technologies.
2. Discuss how AI fosters global connectivity using a specific example.
3. What are the risks associated with the growing reliance on AI?

Section 3: Preparing for the AI-Driven Future

3.1 Opportunities for Individuals

- Upskill in areas like AI development, data science, and ethical AI.
- Leverage online platforms such as **Coursera**, **edX**, and **Skill India** for AI-related certifications.

3.2 Strategies for Organizations

- Adopt AI tools to enhance efficiency and innovation.
- Invest in research and development for integrating emerging AI technologies.

Case Study:

- Tata Consultancy Services (TCS) integrates generative AI to streamline business operations and enhance client services.

o   *Policy and Global Cooperation*

- **India's National Strategy on AI** focuses on AI innovation for inclusive growth.
- Global partnerships, such as the **AI Partnership on the Future of Work**, address challenges like job automation.

Quick Assessment Quiz

1. Name two ways individuals can prepare for an AI-driven future.
2. How can organizations effectively integrate emerging AI technologies?
3. What role do policies play in addressing the challenges of AI adoption?

Chapter Summary

This chapter explored the future of AI by examining emerging trends like generative AI, quantum computing, and autonomous systems. We discussed their potential applications, challenges, and societal impacts. Strategies for individuals and organizations to harness these trends were highlighted, along with the importance of global cooperation in navigating AI's future.

Points to Ponder

1. How will generative AI shape creative industries in the next decade?
2. Are societies prepared for the ethical dilemmas posed by autonomous systems?
3. What steps can governments take to make quantum computing accessible?

Preview of Chapter 9: AI for Good: Solving Global Challenges with Technology

In **Chapter 9**, we will examine how AI addresses global challenges, including climate change, healthcare disparities, and poverty. We'll explore real-world applications and the role of collaboration in achieving sustainable development goals.

References

1. Rephrase.ai - Rephrase.ai
2. Indian Quantum Mission - Quantum Mission
3. AI4Bharat Initiative - AI4Bharat
4. Practo - Practo
5. National Strategy on AI - NITI Aayog AI Strategy
6. Tata Consultancy Services AI Solutions - TCS

Chapter Review Quiz

1. Describe three emerging AI trends and their applications.
2. What are the societal implications of autonomous systems?
3. Name two Indian initiatives promoting AI advancements.
4. Discuss strategies for individuals and organizations to adapt to AI's future.

CHAPTER 9

AI for Good: Solving Global Challenges with Technology

Learning Objectives

By the end of this chapter, you will:

1. Understand how AI addresses global challenges like climate change, poverty, and healthcare disparities.
2. Explore real-world applications of AI in solving social, economic, and environmental problems.
3. Identify the role of partnerships and collaborations in driving AI for good.
4. Discuss ethical and practical considerations when applying AI for global impact.

Recap of Previous Chapter

In Chapter 8, we explored emerging AI trends like generative AI, quantum computing, and autonomous systems. We analyzed their potential to revolutionize industries and society while addressing challenges like ethical dilemmas and implementation barriers.

Section 1: The Role of AI in Addressing Global Challenges

1.1 Tackling Climate Change

AI technologies are being used to predict climate patterns, optimize energy use, and reduce emissions.

Applications:

- AI-powered systems like **IBM's Green Horizon Project** predict air pollution levels and suggest reduction strategies.
- In India, **Tata Power** uses AI to optimize solar energy generation and grid management.

Challenges:

- Data availability and accuracy in underdeveloped regions.
- High energy consumption of AI systems.

1.2 Reducing Poverty and Inequality

AI tools provide insights into socioeconomic patterns, enabling targeted interventions for marginalized communities.

Applications:

- In Kenya, AI is used to identify underserved regions needing infrastructure.
- India's **Aadhaar system**, integrated with AI, enhances the delivery of welfare programs like food distribution.

Challenges:

- Ensuring inclusivity and preventing algorithmic biases that might exacerbate inequality.

1.3 Enhancing Healthcare Access

AI revolutionizes diagnostics, treatment planning, and resource allocation in healthcare.

Applications:

- AI platforms like **Qure.ai** assist Indian radiologists in diagnosing tuberculosis and COVID-19.
- Chatbots like **Ada Health** provide affordable virtual consultations globally.

Quick Assessment Quiz

1. How does AI help tackle climate change?
2. Provide an example of AI reducing poverty in India.
3. Name one AI tool enhancing healthcare in underserved regions.

Section 2: AI Applications for Sustainable Development

2.1 AI and the UN's Sustainable Development Goals (SDGs)

AI aligns with SDGs by addressing issues like zero hunger, quality education, and clean energy.

Examples:

- **Zero Hunger**: AI-powered agricultural tools like **CropIn** improve farming productivity in India.
- **Quality Education**: AI-based platforms like **BYJU'S** provide personalized learning experiences for students.

2.2 Empowering Nonprofits and Governments

AI helps nonprofits and governments make data-driven decisions for impactful interventions.

Case Study:

- The **Bill & Melinda Gates Foundation** uses AI to track the spread of infectious diseases and design vaccination programs.

Quick Assessment Quiz

1. Name two SDGs where AI has made significant contributions.
2. How can AI empower nonprofits in making impactful decisions?

Section 3: Ethical and Practical Considerations

3.1 Ensuring Fair Access to AI

Efforts must be made to make AI accessible and affordable for underserved regions.

Initiative:

- The **AI for All** initiative by the Indian government aims to democratize AI education and access.

3.2 Mitigating Risks of AI Misuse

AI's potential misuse in surveillance, discrimination, or spreading misinformation requires strong regulatory frameworks.

Example:

- The EU's **Artificial Intelligence Act** provides guidelines for ethical AI use.

3.3 Fostering Collaborative Efforts

Collaboration among governments, academia, and private sectors is crucial for scaling AI solutions effectively.

Case Study:

- The **Global Partnership on Artificial Intelligence (GPAI)** brings together multiple stakeholders to ensure AI benefits everyone.

Quick Assessment Quiz

1. Describe the importance of fair access to AI.
2. What are the risks associated with AI misuse?
3. Why is collaboration essential for AI to achieve its full potential?

Chapter Summary

This chapter demonstrated how AI addresses global challenges such as climate change, poverty, and healthcare disparities. We explored AI's alignment with the UN's Sustainable Development Goals and discussed its applications in empowering nonprofits and governments. Ethical considerations and collaborative efforts for scaling AI solutions were also highlighted.

Points to Ponder

1. How can AI contribute to sustainable development while being energy efficient?
2. Are current regulations sufficient to mitigate AI misuse?
3. What role can individuals and organizations play in promoting AI for good?

Preview of Chapter 10: Practical Tips for Adapting to an AI-Driven World

In **Chapter 10**, we will explore actionable strategies for individuals and businesses to thrive in an AI-driven world. Topics include upskilling, embracing AI tools, and staying updated with emerging trends.

References

1. IBM Green Horizon Project - IBM Green Horizon
2. Qure.ai - Qure.ai
3. CropIn - CropIn Technology
4. Bill & Melinda Gates Foundation - Gates Foundation
5. EU Artificial Intelligence Act - AI Act
6. Global Partnership on AI - GPAI

Chapter Review Quiz

1. Name three global challenges AI helps address.
2. How does AI align with the UN's SDGs? Provide examples.
3. Discuss the importance of ethical AI and fair access.
4. What role does collaboration play in scaling AI solutions?

CHAPTER 10

Practical Tips for Adapting to an AI-Driven World

Learning Objectives

By the end of this chapter, you will:

1. Understand the importance of upskilling and lifelong learning in an AI-driven world.
2. Discover practical ways to embrace and integrate AI tools into your personal and professional life.
3. Learn strategies for staying updated with emerging AI trends and technologies.
4. Explore actionable steps to adapt to the changing dynamics of work and life influenced by AI.

Recap of Previous Chapter

In Chapter 9, we discussed how AI addresses global challenges such as climate change, poverty, and healthcare disparities. We explored its alignment with the UN's Sustainable Development Goals and the role of ethical practices and collaboration in ensuring AI benefits all.

Section 1: Upskilling for an AI-Driven Future

1.1 Identifying Skills in Demand

To thrive in an AI-driven world, individuals must focus on developing both technical and soft skills:

- **Technical Skills**: Data analysis, machine learning, coding (e.g., Python, R), and AI ethics.
- **Soft Skills**: Creativity, problem-solving, critical thinking, and adaptability.

Indian Example:

- Programs like **Skill India** offer courses in AI and data science to equip individuals with relevant skills.

Quick Tips:

1. Start with beginner-friendly platforms like **Coursera**, **edX**, and **Udemy**.
2. Pursue certifications in AI-related domains (e.g., Google AI, Microsoft AI Fundamentals).

Challenges:

- Access to affordable and high-quality training resources in underserved areas.

Quick Assessment Quiz

1. What are two technical and soft skills crucial for an AI-driven world?
2. Name one initiative in India supporting AI upskilling.

Section 2: Embracing AI Tools in Daily Life

2.1 AI Tools for Personal Productivity

- **Task Management**:
  Tools like **Notion** and **Todoist** use AI to streamline task organization.
- **Virtual Assistants**: AI-powered assistants like **Google Assistant**, **Alexa**, and **Siri** enhance efficiency.

Indian Example:

AI-powered apps like **DigiLocker** simplify document management for Indian citizens.

AI in Professional Settings

- **Automation**: Tools like **Zapier** automate repetitive tasks, saving time.

- **Data Analysis**: Platforms like **Tableau** and **Power BI** help visualize complex data for decision-making.
- **Collaboration**: AI-driven tools like **Slack** and **Microsoft Teams** enhance team communication.

Case Study:

- **HDFC Bank** uses AI-powered chatbots to provide 24/7 customer support, improving user experience and operational efficiency.

Quick Assessment Quiz

1. List two AI tools for personal productivity and their applications.
2. How do AI-powered platforms like Tableau enhance professional work environments?

Section 3: Staying Updated with AI Trends

3.1 Sources for Staying Informed

- **Online Courses**: Regularly upgrade your knowledge through platforms like **LinkedIn Learning** and **Kaggle**.
- **News and Publications**: Follow AI-focused websites like **AI News** and **TechCrunch AI**.
- **Communities and Events**: Join AI forums and attend webinars, meetups, or conferences (e.g., **AI India Summit**).

3.2 Building a Learning Network

- Collaborate with peers on AI-related projects through platforms like **GitHub**.
- Leverage LinkedIn to connect with AI professionals and thought leaders.

Case Study:

- **TCS iON** provides free AI learning modules to students, making knowledge accessible and fostering a learning community.

Quick Assessment Quiz

1. Name three reliable sources for staying updated with AI trends.
2. Why is building a learning network important in adapting to AI?

Section 4: Adapting to Changes in Work Dynamics

4.1 Reshaping Roles and Industries

AI is redefining job roles, automating routine tasks, and creating new career opportunities.

Examples:

- **Healthcare**: AI tools like **Watson Health** assist in diagnosis and treatment planning.
- **Education**: AI platforms such as **Khan Academy** provide personalized learning experiences.

- *Strategies for Adapting*

- Embrace a growth mindset and seek opportunities to learn continuously.
- Develop hybrid skills that combine domain expertise with AI knowledge.

Indian Example:

- The National AI Mission by NITI Aayog encourages industries to integrate AI for enhanced productivity.

Quick Assessment Quiz

1. How is AI reshaping job roles in industries like healthcare and education?

2. Mention two strategies for individuals to adapt to AI-driven changes in work dynamics.

Chapter Summary

This chapter provided practical tips for adapting to an AI-driven world, focusing on upskilling, integrating AI tools into daily life, staying updated with trends, and preparing for shifts in work dynamics. We explored actionable strategies, highlighted real-world applications, and discussed the importance of continuous learning.

Points to Ponder

1. What steps can you take today to begin your AI learning journey?
2. How can businesses integrate AI tools without disrupting their workflows?
3. Are current educational systems preparing students adequately for an AI-driven future?

Preview of Chapter 11: AI in Health and Medicine: Revolutionizing Patient Care

In **Chapter 11**, we will explore how AI is transforming healthcare through advanced diagnostics, personalized treatment, and operational efficiency. Case studies and ethical considerations will also be examined.

References

1. Coursera AI Courses - Coursera
2. Skill India - Skill India
3. Tableau - Tableau
4. AI News - AI News
5. TCS iON Learning - TCS iON
6. NITI Aayog National AI Mission - National AI Mission

Chapter Review Quiz

1. What are three key skills needed to thrive in an AI-driven world?
2. Name two AI tools for professional productivity and their applications.
3. List three reliable sources for staying informed about AI trends.
4. How can individuals adapt to the changing dynamics of work influenced by AI?

CHAPTER 11

AI in Health and Medicine: Revolutionizing Patient Care

Learning Objectives

By the end of this chapter, you will:

1. Understand the transformative potential of AI in healthcare systems.
2. Explore AI applications in diagnostics, personalized medicine, and drug discovery.
3. Analyze how AI-driven solutions improve operational efficiency in healthcare institutions.
4. Discuss ethical and regulatory challenges associated with AI in healthcare.

Recap of Previous Chapter

In Chapter 10, we explored practical tips for adapting to an AI-driven world. We discussed strategies for individuals and organizations to leverage AI for career growth, effective decision-making, and navigating societal transformations.

Section 1: AI Applications in Diagnostics

1.1 Transforming Diagnostics with AI

AI has dramatically enhanced diagnostic accuracy and speed. AI-powered tools analyze medical images, detect anomalies, and assist clinicians in providing timely interventions.

- **Radiology and Imaging**: AI tools like **Google DeepMind Health** help radiologists interpret X-rays, CT scans, and MRIs with precision, reducing human error and expediting diagnoses.

- **Pathology**: Systems such as **Paige AI** use machine learning algorithms to analyze tissue samples, aiding in early detection of diseases like cancer.
- **Predictive Analytics**: Platforms like **BlueDot** monitor real-time global data to predict disease outbreaks, such as dengue or influenza, facilitating rapid public health responses.

Indian Example:

- **Niramai**, an innovative Indian startup, leverages AI and thermal imaging to detect breast cancer early, offering a radiation-free and affordable diagnostic method.

Expanded Case Study: COVID-19 Pandemic

AI tools were extensively used during the pandemic:

- **CT Scan Analysis**: AI systems differentiated between COVID-19 pneumonia and other lung infections with high accuracy.
- **Contact Tracing**: Apps like **Aarogya Setu** in India utilized AI to track potential exposures and provide timely alerts.

Quick Assessment Quiz

1. How has AI improved diagnostic imaging processes?
2. Name an Indian startup revolutionizing cancer diagnostics using AI.
3. Describe how AI contributed during the COVID-19 pandemic.

Section 2: Personalized Medicine

2.1 Advancing Individualized Treatments

Personalized medicine uses AI to design treatment strategies tailored to an individual's genetic makeup, lifestyle, and medical history.

- **Genomic Data Analysis**: AI tools like **IBM Watson Genomics** analyze genetic profiles to recommend precise therapies for conditions like cancer.
- **Real-Time Monitoring**: Devices such as the **Apple Watch** and **Fitbit** collect health metrics (heart rate, oxygen levels, etc.) and provide actionable insights.
- **Adaptive Treatment Plans**: Platforms like **Ada Health** offer dynamic treatment recommendations based on evolving patient data.

Indian Example:

- **Apollo Hospitals** integrates AI for creating tailored treatment plans, enabling better disease management and improved patient outcomes.

Expanded Case Study: AI for Chronic Diseases

AI is instrumental in managing chronic illnesses:

- **Diabetes**: Apps like **MySugr** use AI to analyze blood sugar trends and suggest lifestyle adjustments.
- **Hypertension**: Wearables track blood pressure levels and alert users to take preventive action.

Quick Assessment Quiz

1. How does AI contribute to genomics in healthcare?
2. Provide two examples of AI-powered devices used for real-time health monitoring.
3. Discuss AI's role in managing chronic diseases like diabetes.

Section 3: Drug Discovery and Development

3.1 Accelerating Drug Discovery

AI has revolutionized the pharmaceutical industry by significantly reducing the time and cost required for drug discovery and clinical trials:

- **Drug Design**: Tools like **Atomwise** leverage AI to screen millions of compounds, identifying potential drugs faster.
- **Preclinical Testing**: AI models predict drug toxicity and efficacy, streamlining preclinical stages.
- **Clinical Trials**: AI helps identify suitable trial participants and optimizes study designs for better outcomes.

Indian Example:

- Companies like **TCS (Tata Consultancy Services)** partner with global pharmaceutical giants to integrate AI in drug discovery, expediting research timelines.

Expanded Challenges

- **Data Integration**: Aggregating data from diverse sources remains complex.
- **Regulatory Bottlenecks**: Ensuring AI-generated insights meet global compliance standards is challenging.

Quick Assessment Quiz

1. How does AI accelerate drug discovery?
2. Name an AI platform that identifies drug compounds efficiently.
3. What are the key challenges in integrating AI into pharmaceutical research?

Section 4: Operational Efficiency in Healthcare

4.1 Enhancing Hospital Operations

AI optimizes administrative and operational tasks in healthcare institutions:

- **Staff Scheduling**: Platforms like **Qventus** predict patient inflow and optimize staffing levels.

- **Appointment Management**: AI-powered chatbots simplify appointment scheduling and patient communication.
- **Resource Allocation**: Predictive analytics ensures efficient utilization of hospital resources such as ICU beds and ventilators.

Indian Example:

- **Manipal Hospitals** employs AI-driven systems to improve patient flow, reduce wait times, and enhance operational efficiency.

- *Expanded Financial Benefits*

- AI reduces healthcare costs by:

- Preventing equipment breakdowns through predictive maintenance.
- Minimizing human errors in billing and record-keeping.

Quick Assessment Quiz

1. How does AI improve staff scheduling in hospitals?
2. Name one Indian hospital that uses AI to enhance operational efficiency.

Section 5: Ethical and Regulatory Considerations

5.1 Ethical Challenges

Ethical concerns surrounding AI in healthcare include:

- **Algorithmic Bias**: Biased datasets can lead to discriminatory outcomes, especially for underrepresented groups.
- **Patient Privacy**: Protecting sensitive health data from unauthorized access is critical.
- **Human Oversight**: Balancing AI automation with human decision-making ensures accountability.

5.2 Regulatory Frameworks

Countries worldwide are developing guidelines to regulate AI usage in healthcare:

- **India**: The Ministry of Health is crafting policies for the safe deployment of AI in medical devices.
- **Global**: Organizations like the WHO and the EU have released frameworks emphasizing data security and ethical AI practices.

Quick Assessment Quiz

1. What are two major ethical challenges associated with AI in healthcare?
2. Name a global organization providing guidelines for ethical AI use.

Chapter Summary

This chapter explored AI's impact on health and medicine, from improving diagnostics and personalized treatments to revolutionizing drug discovery and operational efficiency. Challenges like algorithmic bias and patient privacy were also highlighted, alongside regulatory frameworks shaping the future of AI in healthcare.

Points to Ponder

1. Can AI completely replace doctors in diagnostic roles?
2. What safeguards should be in place to prevent AI-driven healthcare discrimination?
3. How can developing countries benefit from AI in healthcare without significant infrastructure?

Preview of Chapter 12: AI and Education: Shaping the Future of Learning

In **Chapter 12**, we'll explore how AI is transforming education by personalizing learning experiences, enabling smart content creation, and supporting educators through administrative efficiencies.

References

1. Niramai - Niramai
2. Google DeepMind - DeepMind Health
3. IBM Watson Genomics - IBM Watson Genomics
4. Atomwise - Atomwise
5. WHO AI Ethics - WHO AI Guidelines

Chapter Review Quiz

1. Discuss three ways AI enhances healthcare diagnostics.
2. Explain the role of AI in managing chronic diseases.
3. What are the main financial benefits of using AI in healthcare operations?
4. Identify two ethical concerns related to AI and suggest solutions.
5. How do AI-powered tools streamline hospital administration?

CHAPTER 12

AI and Education: Shaping the Future of Learning

Learning Objectives

By the end of this chapter, you will:

1. Understand how AI is transforming the education sector through personalization and smart tools.
2. Explore AI applications in administrative efficiency and curriculum enhancement.
3. Discuss the ethical and practical considerations of adopting AI in education.
4. Identify emerging trends and future possibilities in AI-powered education systems.

Recap of Previous Chapter

In Chapter 11, we discussed the transformative impact of AI in health and medicine, exploring its applications in diagnostics, personalized medicine, and operational efficiency. The chapter also covered ethical challenges and regulatory frameworks shaping AI's role in healthcare.

Section 1: Personalized Learning Experiences

1.1 Customizing Education for Individual Needs

AI enables personalized education tailored to students' learning styles, strengths, and weaknesses.

- **Adaptive Learning Platforms**: Tools like **DreamBox Learning** and **BYJU'S (India)** adapt lesson plans in real time based on a student's progress.

- **Intelligent Tutoring Systems**: AI tutors provide instant feedback, such as **Socratic by Google**, which uses AI to help students solve problems interactively.
- **Skill Assessments**: Platforms like **Knewton** analyze learning behaviors and recommend courses to bridge skill gaps.

Indian Example:

- **BYJU'S**, India's largest ed-tech company, uses AI to provide interactive and personalized learning experiences for millions of students globally.

Quick Assessment Quiz

1. What is adaptive learning, and how does it benefit students?
2. Name an AI-powered tutoring system that provides real-time feedback.
3. How does BYJU'S integrate AI into its platform?

Section 2: Smart Content Creation and Delivery

2.1 Enhancing Learning Materials with AI

AI-powered tools simplify and enhance content creation for educators:

- **Digital Textbooks**: Platforms like **Content Technologies, Inc.** generate personalized textbooks from existing content.
- **Virtual Labs**: Tools such as **Labster** simulate lab environments, allowing students to conduct experiments virtually.
- **Interactive Assessments**: AI systems create tailored quizzes and assignments to reinforce learning.

Indian Example:

- **Vedantu** uses AI to analyze student performance and deliver targeted study materials, improving learning outcomes.

Expanded Use of AI in Interactive Learning

- **Gamification**: AI systems add game-like elements to lessons, boosting engagement.
- **Language Translation**: Tools like **Duolingo** use AI to personalize language learning journeys.

Quick Assessment Quiz

1. Name two tools that assist in digital content creation for education.
2. How do virtual labs improve practical learning for students?
3. Discuss how AI gamification enhances student engagement.

Section 3: Supporting Educators with AI Tools

3.1 Streamlining Administrative Tasks

AI reduces the administrative burden on educators, allowing them to focus more on teaching:

- **Automated Grading**: Systems like **Gradescope** assess assignments, saving time for teachers.
- **Attendance Management**: AI-powered attendance systems streamline classroom operations.
- **Course Design**: AI tools like **Coursera's AI Analytics** help educators optimize course structure.

Indian Example:

- **Shiksha AI** offers Indian educators AI-driven insights to improve lesson plans and manage administrative tasks effectively.

Expanded Role of AI in Professional Development

AI provides educators with continuous learning opportunities:

- Access to online courses tailored to their teaching needs.
- Feedback-driven improvement plans generated through AI analytics.

Quick Assessment Quiz

1. What is the primary benefit of automated grading for educators?
2. Name an AI tool that optimizes course design.
3. How does AI support teachers' professional development?

Section 4: Ethical Considerations in AI-Driven Education

4.1 Addressing Concerns and Challenges

The widespread adoption of AI in education brings ethical challenges:

- **Data Privacy**: Protecting students' personal data from misuse is a key concern.
- **Equity in Access**: Ensuring AI tools are available to students in underprivileged areas is crucial.
- **Teacher Dependency**: Striking a balance between human educators and AI assistance is necessary.

Indian Challenges

India faces unique challenges such as:

- Limited digital infrastructure in rural areas.
- High costs of advanced AI tools for smaller schools.

1. What are the ethical challenges associated with AI in education?
2. Discuss the challenges India faces in adopting AI for education.
3. How can schools ensure data privacy while using AI tools?

Section 5: Emerging Trends in AI and Education

5.1 The Future of AI-Powered Learning

AI is paving the way for innovative trends in education:

- **Immersive Learning**: AR/VR combined with AI provides immersive classroom experiences.
- **Predictive Analytics**: AI predicts student performance and suggests interventions for improvement.
- **Global Classrooms**: AI-powered translation tools facilitate seamless global collaboration among students.

Expanded Global Examples:

- **EdTech Platforms**: Platforms like **Khan Academy** use AI to deliver free and quality education globally.
- **AI in Exams**: Tools like **Proctorio** ensure fair and unbiased online assessments.

Quick Assessment Quiz

1. What are the key emerging trends in AI for education?
2. Name an example of AI-powered immersive learning.
3. How do global classrooms benefit from AI-driven tools?

Chapter Summary

In this chapter, we explored AI's transformative role in education. From personalized learning and content creation to supporting educators and addressing ethical challenges, AI is revolutionizing how knowledge is imparted and consumed. The future of education, driven by AI, promises inclusivity, innovation, and improved accessibility.

Points to Ponder

1. How can AI help bridge the educational gap in rural areas?
2. Should educators be fully reliant on AI tools for teaching? Why or why not?
3. How can governments ensure equal access to AI-powered education systems?

Preview of Chapter 13: AI in Sustainability: Driving Green Innovations

In **Chapter 13**, we will explore how AI is shaping sustainable solutions for environmental challenges, including smart energy systems, waste management, and climate change mitigation.

References

1. DreamBox Learning - DreamBox
2. BYJU'S - BYJU'S
3. Labster - Labster
4. Gradescope - Gradescope
5. Khan Academy - Khan Academy

Chapter Review Quiz

1. Define adaptive learning and its benefits.
2. Discuss the ethical challenges of AI in education.
3. How do tools like virtual labs transform practical learning?

4. What emerging trends in AI will shape the future of education?
5. Explain the role of AI in administrative tasks for educators.

CHAPTER 13

AI in Sustainability: Driving Green Innovations

Learning Objectives

By the end of this chapter, you will:

1. Understand the role of AI in addressing global environmental challenges.
2. Explore AI-driven solutions for energy efficiency, waste management, and sustainable urban planning.
3. Learn about the integration of AI in tackling climate change and biodiversity conservation.
4. Discuss the challenges and ethical considerations of applying AI in sustainability initiatives.

Recap of Previous Chapter

In Chapter 12, we examined how AI is revolutionizing education through personalized learning, content creation, and administrative support. Ethical challenges, such as data privacy and equitable access, were discussed, along with emerging trends like immersive learning and predictive analytics.

Section 1: AI for Energy Efficiency

1.1 Optimizing Energy Consumption

AI plays a significant role in reducing energy wastage and improving efficiency in various sectors:

- **Smart Grids**: AI-powered grids monitor and distribute electricity based on real-time demand.
    - Example: **Siemens Spectrum Power** utilizes AI to manage energy distribution effectively.
- **Building Automation**: AI systems like **Honeywell Forge** optimize energy use in buildings by analyzing

patterns and controlling systems like HVAC and lighting.

- *Indian Example:*
- **Tata Power Delhi Distribution Limited** employs AI-driven smart grids to minimize power outages and improve energy efficiency.

Quick Assessment Quiz

1. What is the role of AI in smart grids?
2. Name an AI system that optimizes energy use in buildings.
3. How does Tata Power Delhi Distribution Limited use AI for energy efficiency?

Section 2: AI in Waste Management

2.1 Revolutionizing Waste Sorting and Recycling

AI technologies streamline waste management processes:

- **Automated Waste Sorting**: Systems like **ZenRobotics** identify and sort materials for recycling using AI vision.
- **Predictive Waste Management**: Tools predict waste generation patterns and optimize collection schedules.

2.2 Reducing Landfill Impact

AI models identify sustainable alternatives to landfilling by improving recycling rates and designing circular economy strategies.

Indian Example:

- **Banyan Nation**, an Indian startup, uses AI to track and improve plastic recycling efforts.

Quick Assessment Quiz

1. How does AI automate waste sorting processes?

2. Name an AI startup in India focusing on recycling plastics.
3. Discuss the role of AI in reducing landfill impact.

Section 3: AI for Sustainable Urban Planning

3.1 Smart Cities and Sustainable Development

AI enables the development of smart, eco-friendly cities:

- **Traffic Management**: AI tools like **INRIX Traffic Intelligence** reduce congestion and emissions.
- **Water Management**: AI-powered systems predict and manage water usage to prevent wastage.
- **Urban Forest Management**: Tools like **Treepedia** assess urban greenery levels to enhance environmental planning.

Indian Example:

- **Smart City Mission** in India uses AI for efficient urban infrastructure and resource management.

Quick Assessment Quiz

1. What are the applications of AI in urban planning?
2. How does the Smart City Mission in India leverage AI?
3. Name an AI tool that supports urban greenery assessment.

Section 4: Tackling Climate Change with AI

4.1 Climate Modeling and Predictions

AI systems analyze large datasets to predict climate patterns:

- **Weather Forecasting**: Tools like **IBM's Deep Thunder** provide hyper-local weather forecasts.
- **Disaster Management**: AI aids in predicting natural disasters like floods and hurricanes.

- *Carbon Footprint Reduction*

- AI identifies sources of carbon emissions and suggests reduction strategies:

- **Energy Transition Planning**: AI models optimize renewable energy integration into grids.

- *Indian Example:*

- **WRI India** uses AI to analyze carbon emissions and suggest urban solutions to reduce environmental impact.

Quick Assessment Quiz

1. How does AI contribute to weather forecasting?
2. Discuss AI's role in disaster management.
3. Provide an example of an Indian organization using AI for climate change mitigation.

Section 5: Biodiversity and Ecosystem Conservation

5.1 Monitoring Wildlife and Ecosystems

AI assists in preserving biodiversity by:

- **Camera Traps**: AI-powered systems like **Wildbook** identify species and track wildlife populations.
- **Deforestation Detection**: AI tools analyze satellite imagery to detect and prevent deforestation.

    Indian Example:

- **Wildlife Institute of India** uses AI to monitor tiger populations and combat poaching.

Quick Assessment Quiz

1. What is Wildbook, and how does it help in biodiversity conservation?
2. Discuss how AI detects deforestation.

3. How is AI used by the Wildlife Institute of India?

Section 6: Challenges and Ethical Considerations

6.1 Barriers to AI Adoption in Sustainability

- **High Costs**: AI infrastructure can be expensive for developing countries.
- **Data Availability**: Lack of reliable datasets limits AI's effectiveness.

6.2 Ethical Issues

- **Bias in AI Models**: Inaccurate predictions may lead to unintended environmental consequences.
- **Access Disparity**: Ensuring equitable access to AI-powered sustainability solutions is vital.

Quick Assessment Quiz

1. What are the key barriers to adopting AI in sustainability?
2. Discuss ethical concerns related to AI in environmental applications.
3. How can countries address the issue of access disparity in AI solutions?

Chapter Summary

This chapter highlighted AI's transformative potential in driving sustainability across energy, waste management, urban planning, climate change mitigation, and biodiversity conservation. While the opportunities are vast, challenges such as ethical concerns and resource availability need attention to maximize AI's impact.

Points to Ponder

1. How can AI help improve recycling efficiency in urban areas?
2. Should governments prioritize AI funding for sustainability? Why or why not?

3. What role can citizens play in supporting AI-driven sustainability initiatives?

Preview of Chapter 14: AI in Entertainment: Redefining Creativity and Engagement

In **Chapter 14**, we will explore AI's role in transforming the entertainment industry, from content creation to personalized user experiences and ethical challenges in media automation.

References

1. Siemens Spectrum Power - Click Here
2. ZenRobotics - Click Here
3. Honeywell Forge - Click Here
4. Banyan Nation - Click Here
5. Wildbook - Click Here
6. INRIX Traffic Intelligence - Click Here

Chapter Review Quiz

1. Define the role of AI in optimizing energy efficiency.
2. How does AI assist in waste management?
3. Discuss the ethical concerns related to AI in sustainability initiatives.
4. Provide examples of AI tools used in biodiversity conservation.
5. What are the emerging trends in AI for sustainable urban development?

CHAPTER 14

AI in Entertainment: Redefining Creativity and Engagement

Learning Objectives

By the end of this chapter, you will:

1. Understand how AI is transforming the entertainment industry.
2. Explore AI applications in content creation, recommendation systems, and audience engagement.
3. Analyze the ethical challenges associated with AI in entertainment.
4. Learn about emerging trends in AI-powered entertainment technologies.

Recap of Previous Chapter

In Chapter 13, we explored how AI is driving sustainability by optimizing energy consumption, improving waste management, supporting urban planning, mitigating climate change, and conserving biodiversity. Challenges such as ethical concerns and access disparities were also discussed.

Section 1: AI in Content Creation

1.1 Generating Content with AI

AI has revolutionized content creation by automating repetitive tasks and enhancing creativity:

- **Video Production**: AI tools like **RunwayML** assist in editing and creating video content.
- **Music Composition**: Platforms such as **AIVA (Artificial Intelligence Virtual Artist)** generate music tailored to user preferences.

- **Scriptwriting**: AI systems analyze existing scripts to suggest plotlines, dialogues, and character development.

1.2 Visual Effects and Animation

AI-powered tools streamline visual effects and animation processes, enabling faster production:

- **Deep Learning Models**: Used in de-aging actors or creating hyper-realistic CGI characters.
- Example: AI in Marvel Studios' *Avengers: Endgame* for de-aging actors.

Quick Assessment Quiz

1. Name an AI tool used for video editing.
2. How does AI assist in music composition?
3. What are some applications of AI in visual effects and animation?

Section 2: Personalized User Experiences

2.1 Recommendation Systems

AI algorithms curate personalized recommendations to enhance user satisfaction:

- **Streaming Platforms**: Netflix and Spotify use AI to recommend shows, movies, and music based on user preferences.
- **Gaming**: AI personalizes gaming experiences through dynamic difficulty adjustment and adaptive storytelling.

2.2 Immersive Experiences

AI technologies power interactive and immersive entertainment:

- **Virtual Reality (VR)**: AI enhances VR experiences by simulating realistic environments.

- **Augmented Reality (AR)**: Applications like **Pokémon GO** integrate AI to create engaging AR experiences.

Indian Example:

- **Gaana** uses AI to deliver personalized music playlists to its users based on listening habits.

Quick Assessment Quiz

1. How does AI improve user experiences on streaming platforms?

2. Discuss the role of AI in immersive entertainment.

3. Provide an example of an Indian company using AI for personalized recommendations.

Section 3: AI in Audience Engagement

3.1 Real-Time Interaction

AI-powered chatbots and virtual assistants engage audiences dynamically:

- **Example**: Virtual influencers like **Lil Miquela** interact with followers on social media platforms.
- **Live Streaming**: AI analyzes audience reactions in real time to optimize content delivery.

3.2 Sentiment Analysis

AI tools analyze audience feedback to improve content strategies:

- **Social Media Monitoring**: Tools like **Hootsuite Insights** analyze viewer sentiment to tailor campaigns.

Quick Assessment Quiz

1. What are virtual influencers, and how do they engage audiences?
2. How does AI support sentiment analysis for content improvement?
3. Name a tool that helps monitor audience feedback on social media.

Section 4: Ethical Challenges of AI in Entertainment

4.1 Deepfake Risks

AI-powered deepfake technology raises concerns about misinformation and misuse:

- **Example**: Deepfakes in celebrity endorsements or fake news creation.

4.2 Bias in Algorithms

AI systems may reinforce biases in content recommendations:

- **Example**: Recommending similar types of content, reducing exposure to diverse genres.

4.3 Copyright and Ownership Issues

AI-generated content blurs the lines of intellectual property rights:

- Who owns the rights to music or videos created entirely by AI?

Quick Assessment Quiz

1. What are the ethical concerns surrounding AI in entertainment?
2. Discuss the potential misuse of deepfake technology.
3. How can AI bias affect content diversity?

Section 5: Emerging Trends in AI Entertainment

5.1 Generative AI in Creativity

- Tools like **ChatGPT** and **DALL-E** are used for scriptwriting, concept art, and design.

5.2 AI-Driven Interactive Storytelling

- AI enables real-time adjustments to storylines based on user input in games or interactive shows.

5.3 Blockchain Integration

- AI integrates with blockchain for secure distribution of digital content.

Quick Assessment Quiz

1. What is generative AI, and how is it used in entertainment?
2. Discuss the role of AI in interactive storytelling.
3. How does blockchain complement AI in the entertainment industry?

Chapter Summary

This chapter explored how AI is transforming the entertainment industry through content creation, personalized user experiences, and audience engagement. Ethical challenges, such as deepfake risks and copyright issues, were addressed, alongside emerging trends like generative AI and blockchain integration.

Points to Ponder

1. Can AI replace human creativity in entertainment? Why or why not?
2. How should industries address ethical challenges like deepfake misuse?
3. What future innovations do you foresee in AI-powered entertainment?

Preview of Chapter 15: AI in Finance: Smart Solutions for Money Management

In **Chapter 15**, we will delve into AI's role in revolutionizing the finance industry, from fraud detection and personalized banking to algorithmic trading and financial planning.

References

1. RunwayML - Click Here
2. AIVA - Click Here
3. Netflix Recommendation System - Click Here
4. Hootsuite Insights - Click Here
5. Pokémon GO - Click Here
6. DALL-E - Click Here

Chapter Review Quiz

1. What are the key applications of AI in content creation?
2. How does AI enhance user experiences in the gaming industry?
3. Discuss the ethical challenges of AI in entertainment.
4. What role does blockchain play in AI-powered entertainment?
5. Name two tools that demonstrate emerging trends in AI entertainment.

CHAPTER 15

AI in Finance: Smart Solutions for Money Management

Learning Objectives

By the end of this chapter, you will:

1. Understand the transformative role of AI in the finance industry.
2. Learn how AI enhances fraud detection, algorithmic trading, and financial planning.
3. Explore the ethical and regulatory challenges associated with AI in finance.
4. Discover emerging trends in AI-powered financial technologies.

Recap of Previous Chapter

In Chapter 14, we examined the transformative power of AI in the entertainment industry. From content creation to personalized user experiences, AI is reshaping how audiences consume and interact with media. The chapter also addressed ethical challenges and emerging trends, such as generative AI and blockchain integration.

Section 1: AI in Fraud Detection

1.1 Real-Time Monitoring

AI algorithms analyze transactions in real time to identify potential fraud.

- **Tools Used**:
- **SAS Fraud Management**: Detects anomalies using machine learning models.
- **Feedzai**: Provides end-to-end fraud prevention solutions.

1.2 Behavioral Analysis

AI tracks user behavior to flag unusual activities, such as:

- Sudden large transactions.
- Logging in from unusual locations or devices.
- **Indian Example**: Banks like **HDFC Bank** use AI-powered systems to detect fraudulent activities.

Quick Assessment Quiz

1. Name a tool used for fraud detection in finance.
2. How does AI leverage behavioral analysis to detect fraud?
3. Provide an example of an Indian bank using AI for fraud prevention.

Section 2: AI in Algorithmic Trading

2.1 Speed and Accuracy

AI systems execute trades faster and more accurately by analyzing large datasets in real time:

- **High-Frequency Trading (HFT)**: AI identifies profitable trading opportunities within microseconds.
- **Example**: AI algorithms used by **Goldman Sachs** for stock trading.

2.2 Predictive Analytics

AI predicts market trends by analyzing historical data, news, and social sentiment:

- **Tools Used**:
- **Kavout**: Provides AI-based stock ranking models.
- **Numerai**: A crowdsourced hedge fund using AI.

1. What is high-frequency trading, and how does AI enhance it?
2. Name two tools that use AI for algorithmic trading.
3. How does AI predict market trends?

Section 3: AI in Personalized Banking and Financial Planning

3.1 Chatbots and Virtual Assistants

AI-powered chatbots assist customers with:

- Balance inquiries.
- Transaction details.
- Personalized financial advice.
- **Examples**:
- **SBI's YONO** app integrates AI to provide financial planning tools.
- **Bank of America's Erica** chatbot offers personalized insights.

3.2 Robo-Advisors

AI-driven robo-advisors create customized investment portfolios based on user goals:

- **Tools Used**:
- **Betterment**: Offers goal-based investing.
- **Wealthfront**: Provides automated financial planning.

- *Indian Example:*

- **Paytm Money** uses AI to offer personalized investment recommendations.

Quick Assessment Quiz

1. How do chatbots improve customer experience in banking?
2. What is the role of robo-advisors in financial planning?

3. Name an Indian financial platform using AI for investment recommendations.

Section 4: Ethical and Regulatory Challenges

4.1 Data Privacy Concerns

AI systems handle vast amounts of sensitive financial data, raising concerns about:

- Data breaches.
- Unauthorized access.
- **Example**: The Facebook-Cambridge Analytica scandal highlights potential misuse of user data.

4.2 Bias in AI Models

AI models may inadvertently favor certain demographics, leading to unfair lending practices:

- **Example**: AI loan approval systems rejecting minority applicants due to biased training data.

4.3 Regulatory Challenges

The rapid adoption of AI in finance outpaces regulatory frameworks, leading to:

- Lack of standardized guidelines.
- Potential risks for consumers and institutions.

Quick Assessment Quiz

1. What are the primary data privacy concerns associated with AI in finance?
2. Discuss how bias in AI models can affect lending practices.
3. Why is regulation important for AI in finance?

Section 5: Emerging Trends in AI-Powered Finance

5.1 Blockchain Integration

AI integrates with blockchain to enhance transparency and security in financial transactions:

- **Example**: AI-powered smart contracts for secure and automated payments.

5.2 Explainable AI (XAI)

Explainable AI provides insights into decision-making processes, improving trust and compliance.

5.3 Green Finance

AI supports sustainable investing by identifying eco-friendly investment opportunities.

Quick Assessment Quiz

1. How does AI integrate with blockchain in finance?
2. What is explainable AI, and why is it important in finance?
3. Discuss the role of AI in promoting green finance.

Chapter Summary

This chapter highlighted AI's transformative impact on the finance industry. From fraud detection and algorithmic trading to personalized banking and financial planning, AI is driving efficiency and innovation. Ethical and regulatory challenges, such as data privacy concerns and biases, were discussed alongside emerging trends like blockchain integration and green finance.

Points to Ponder

1. How can financial institutions balance AI innovation with ethical considerations?
2. What steps can be taken to reduce bias in AI-based financial systems?

3. How will explainable AI impact regulatory compliance in the finance sector?

Preview of Chapter 16: AI and Emotional Intelligence: Can Machines Understand Us?

In **Chapter 16**, we will explore AI's potential to understand and respond to human emotions. The chapter will delve into emotion recognition technologies, their applications in various industries, and the ethical implications of AI-driven emotional intelligence.

References

1. SAS Fraud Management - Click Here
2. Feedzai - Click Here
3. Kavout - Click Here
4. Numerai - Click Here
5. SBI YONO - Click Here
6. Betterment - Click Here
7. Wealthfront - Click Here
8. Paytm Money - Click Here
9. Explainable AI (XAI) - Click Here

Chapter Review Quiz

1. Describe the role of AI in fraud detection and provide examples of tools used.
2. What is algorithmic trading, and how does AI contribute to it?
3. Discuss the advantages of AI-driven robo-advisors in financial planning.
4. Identify key ethical and regulatory challenges of AI in finance.
5. Explain the importance of blockchain integration in AI-powered finance.

CHAPTER 16

AI and Emotional Intelligence: Can Machines Understand Us?

Learning Objectives

By the end of this chapter, you will:

1. Understand the concept of emotional intelligence and how it relates to artificial intelligence.
2. Explore the technologies enabling emotion recognition and sentiment analysis.
3. Learn about applications of emotionally intelligent AI across industries.
4. Discuss the ethical concerns and limitations of AI in understanding emotions.
5. Discover emerging trends and future possibilities for emotionally intelligent AI.

Recap of Previous Chapter

In Chapter 15, we explored how AI is revolutionizing the finance industry through fraud detection, algorithmic trading, and personalized financial planning. Ethical and regulatory challenges were examined alongside trends such as blockchain integration and explainable AI.

Section 1: What Is Emotional Intelligence in AI?

1.1 Defining Emotional Intelligence

Emotional intelligence refers to the ability to recognize, understand, and respond to emotions in oneself and others. In AI, it involves:

- Detecting emotional cues from voice, text, and facial expressions.
- Responding empathetically to user inputs.

1.2 Components of Emotionally Intelligent AI

1. **Emotion Recognition**: Identifying emotions through facial recognition, tone analysis, and physiological signals.
2. **Sentiment Analysis**: Interpreting the emotional tone of written or spoken text.
3. **Context Awareness**: Understanding the situational context of emotional expressions.

Quick Assessment Quiz

1. What is emotional intelligence, and how does it apply to AI?
2. Name three components of emotionally intelligent AI.

Section 2: Technologies Behind Emotionally Intelligent AI

2.1 Facial Emotion Recognition

AI systems analyze facial expressions to infer emotions.

- **Tools Used**:
- **Affectiva**: Specializes in emotion AI for facial recognition.
- **Microsoft Azure Face API**: Detects emotions from facial features.

2.2 Sentiment Analysis

AI interprets emotions from text using natural language processing (NLP).

- **Examples**:
- Analyzing customer reviews to determine satisfaction levels.
- Monitoring social media sentiment for brand perception.

2.3 Voice Emotion Analysis

AI analyzes vocal tone, pitch, and rhythm to assess emotions.

- **Tools Used**:
- **NVIDIA Jarvis**: Provides conversational AI capabilities.
- **Cogito**: Enhances emotional intelligence in customer interactions.

Quick Assessment Quiz

1. Name two tools used for facial emotion recognition.
2. How does sentiment analysis work in AI?
3. Provide an example of voice emotion analysis in real-world applications.

Section 3: Applications of Emotionally Intelligent AI

3.1 Healthcare

Emotionally intelligent AI improves mental health support through:

- Chatbots like **Wysa** offering empathetic conversations.
- AI-powered diagnostics for identifying emotional distress.

3.2 Education

AI adapts learning experiences by recognizing students' emotions.

- **Example**: AI tutors that adjust difficulty based on frustration levels.

3.3 Customer Service

AI enhances customer experience by detecting emotions during interactions.

- **Tools**:
- **Zendesk AI**: Tracks customer sentiment to improve support.

3.4 Marketing

AI predicts consumer preferences by analyzing emotional responses to advertisements.

- **Example**: Emotion AI used in campaigns to measure engagement.

Indian Examples

- **Practo**: Incorporates emotion recognition for telehealth consultations.
- AI-enabled student assessment tools in **BYJU'S**

Learning App.

Quick Assessment Quiz

1. How is emotionally intelligent AI used in healthcare?
2. Name an example of emotionally intelligent AI in education.
3. Discuss how AI enhances customer service by recognizing emotions.

Section 4: Ethical Concerns and Limitations

4.1 Privacy Issues

Emotionally intelligent AI collects sensitive personal data, leading to:

- Concerns over misuse of facial and voice data.
- **Example**: Potential misuse of biometric data in unauthorized ways.

4.2 Accuracy and Bias

AI systems may misinterpret emotions due to:

- Cultural differences in emotional expressions.

- Biases in training data.

4.3 Emotional Manipulation

AI could exploit emotions for manipulative marketing or political campaigns.

- **Case Study**: Concerns over emotion-targeted ads on social media platforms.

Quick Assessment Quiz

1. What are the privacy concerns associated with emotionally intelligent AI?
2. How can cultural biases affect emotion recognition?
3. Discuss the ethical implications of using AI for emotional manipulation.

Section 5: Future of Emotionally Intelligent AI

5.1 Enhancing Empathy in Machines

Future AI systems may simulate empathy more convincingly for improved interactions.

5.2 Integration with Wearable Devices

AI could use biometric data from wearables to provide real-time emotional insights.

5.3 Cross-Cultural Emotion Recognition

Advancements in training AI models to recognize culturally diverse emotional expressions.

Quick Assessment Quiz

1. How can AI systems simulate empathy?
2. Discuss the role of wearable devices in emotionally intelligent AI.
3. Why is cross-cultural emotion recognition important?

Chapter Summary

This chapter explored emotionally intelligent AI and its ability to recognize and respond to human emotions. Technologies like facial emotion recognition, sentiment analysis, and voice emotion analysis were discussed alongside applications in healthcare, education, and customer service. Ethical concerns, including privacy issues and potential emotional manipulation, were addressed. Finally, future trends such as empathy simulation and wearable integration were examined.

Points to Ponder

1. Can AI truly understand human emotions, or is it limited to simulations?
2. What steps can organizations take to ensure ethical use of emotionally intelligent AI?
3. How might emotionally intelligent AI impact human relationships in the long term?

Preview of Chapter 17: AI for Entrepreneurs: Launching and Growing Businesses with AI

In **Chapter 17**, we will explore how entrepreneurs can leverage AI to innovate, streamline operations, and scale their businesses. Topics will include AI-driven market research, customer acquisition, and operational efficiency.

References

1. Affectiva - Click Here
2. Microsoft Azure Face API - Click Here
3. NVIDIA Jarvis - Click Here
4. Cogito - Click Here
5. Wysa - Click Here
6. Zendesk AI - Click Here
7. Practo - Click Here
8. BYJU'S Learning App - Click Here

9. Explainable AI (XAI) - Click Here

Chapter Review Quiz

1. Define emotional intelligence in the context of AI.
2. How does sentiment analysis help businesses understand customers?
3. What are the ethical challenges in implementing emotionally intelligent AI?
4. Discuss potential future advancements in emotionally intelligent AI.

CHAPTER 17

AI for Entrepreneurs: Launching and Growing Businesses with AI

Learning Objectives

By the end of this chapter, you will:

1. Understand the role of AI in entrepreneurial innovation and business growth.
2. Explore AI tools for market research, customer acquisition, and operational efficiency.
3. Learn practical strategies for implementing AI in startups and SMEs.
4. Identify challenges and solutions when adopting AI as an entrepreneur.
5. Discover case studies of successful AI-driven businesses.

Recap of Previous Chapter

In Chapter 16, we examined emotionally intelligent AI and its applications in various domains such as healthcare, education, and customer service. We discussed ethical concerns, including privacy and bias, and explored the future of AI systems simulating empathy and integrating with wearable devices.

Section 1: Role of AI in Entrepreneurship

1.1 Redefining Business Models

AI enables entrepreneurs to:

- Automate routine tasks, allowing more focus on strategy and innovation.
- Deliver personalized customer experiences.
- Scale operations faster with data-driven decision-making.

1.2 Democratizing Access to Technology

With affordable cloud solutions and AI-as-a-Service platforms, entrepreneurs now have access to cutting-edge tools without requiring extensive technical expertise.

1.3 Empowering Data-Driven Decisions

AI transforms raw data into actionable insights for decision-making.

- **Example**: Predicting market trends through AI-powered analytics tools.

Quick Assessment Quiz

1. How does AI redefine business models for entrepreneurs?
2. What is the role of AI in data-driven decision-making?
3. Name an AI service that democratizes access to technology.

Section 2: AI Tools for Entrepreneurs

2.1 Market Research

AI tools simplify market research by analyzing consumer behavior, competitor data, and industry trends.

- **Examples**:
- **Semrush**: Analyzes competitor performance and identifies keywords.
- **ThinkWithGoogle**: Provides consumer insights and industry trends.

2.2 Customer Acquisition

AI improves targeting and engagement strategies for entrepreneurs.

- **Tools**:

- **HubSpot**: Automates marketing campaigns with AI insights.
- **Conversica**: Engages leads through AI-driven email and chat.

2.3 Operational Efficiency

AI streamlines processes to reduce costs and improve productivity.

- **Examples**:
- **Zapier**: Automates workflows across apps.
- **UiPath**: Provides robotic process automation (RPA) for repetitive tasks.

Indian Examples

- **Niramai**: Uses AI for breast cancer screening and has scaled operations efficiently.
- **Zolve**: AI-powered financial solutions for global citizens.

Quick Assessment Quiz

1. How does AI enhance market research?
2. Name two tools used for customer acquisition.
3. Provide an example of AI improving operational efficiency.

Section 3: Strategies for Implementing AI in Startups and SMEs

3.1 Start Small, Scale Fast

- Begin with pilot projects in one area of the business.
- Use insights from initial implementations to scale AI applications.

3.2 Partner with AI Providers

Collaborate with established AI companies to leverage their expertise and infrastructure.

3.3 Upskilling Teams

Train employees to work alongside AI systems for a smooth transition.

- **Example**: Conduct workshops on using AI tools like ChatGPT or Tableau.

Quick Assessment Quiz

1. Why is starting small an effective strategy for AI adoption?
2. How can partnering with AI providers benefit entrepreneurs?
3. Why is upskilling teams crucial for AI integration?

Section 4: Challenges and Solutions in Adopting AI

4.1 Limited Budget and Resources

AI implementation can be costly, especially for startups.

- **Solution**: Leverage free or low-cost AI tools and cloud platforms like Google AI and AWS.

4.2 Lack of Expertise

Entrepreneurs may lack technical knowledge to deploy AI effectively.

- **Solution**: Hire consultants or invest in no-code AI platforms.

4.3 Resistance to Change

Employees or stakeholders may resist adopting new technologies.

- **Solution**: Educate teams on the benefits of AI through workshops and demonstrations.

Quick Assessment Quiz

1. How can entrepreneurs overcome budget constraints when implementing AI?

2. What role do no-code AI platforms play in addressing a lack of expertise?
3. How can resistance to AI adoption be mitigated?

Section 5: Case Studies of AI-Driven Businesses

5.1 Case Study: Dunzo (India)

Dunzo uses AI to optimize hyperlocal delivery operations.

- **Impact**: Reduced delivery times and improved customer satisfaction.

5.2 Case Study: Stitch Fix (USA)

This fashion retailer uses AI to recommend personalized clothing options.

- **Impact**: Enhanced customer retention and reduced return rates.

5.3 Case Study: Razorpay (India)

AI-powered payment gateway simplifying online transactions for businesses.

- **Impact**: Accelerated payment processing and fraud detection.

Quick Assessment Quiz

1. How does Dunzo leverage AI for business efficiency?
2. What AI solution does Stitch Fix use for customer retention?
3. Discuss Razorpay's use of AI for payment processing.

Chapter Summary

This chapter outlined how AI empowers entrepreneurs to innovate and scale their businesses. Key tools for market research, customer acquisition, and operational efficiency were explored, along with strategies for AI implementation in startups and SMEs. Challenges such as limited budgets and resistance to change were addressed, supported by practical solutions. Case studies demonstrated the transformative potential of AI in entrepreneurial ventures.

Points to Ponder

1. How can entrepreneurs effectively balance AI implementation costs with expected benefits?
2. What industries have the most potential for AI-driven innovation by startups?
3. How might AI reshape the entrepreneurial landscape in the next decade?

Preview of Chapter 18: AI and Accessibility: Empowering Inclusivity

In **Chapter 18**, we will explore how AI is breaking barriers and empowering individuals with disabilities. Topics will include AI-driven assistive technologies, inclusive design principles, and case studies of successful implementations.

References

1. Semrush - Click Here
2. ThinkWithGoogle - Click Here
3. HubSpot - Click Here
4. Conversica - Click Here
5. Zapier - Click Here
6. UiPath - Click Here
7. Niramai - Click Here
8. Zolve - Click Here
9. Google AI - Click Here
10. AWS AI Services - Click Here

Chapter Review Quiz

1. What are the primary roles of AI in entrepreneurship?

2. Name three AI tools for enhancing operational efficiency.
3. Discuss strategies for overcoming challenges in AI adoption.
4. Provide examples of startups that have successfully implemented AI.

CHAPTER 18

AI and Accessibility: Empowering Inclusivity

Learning Objectives

By the end of this chapter, you will:

1. Understand the significance of AI in promoting accessibility for individuals with disabilities.
2. Explore AI-driven assistive technologies and their real-world applications.
3. Learn about inclusive design principles and their role in technology development.
4. Analyze case studies showcasing AI's impact on inclusivity.
5. Identify the challenges and ethical considerations in using AI for accessibility.

Recap of Previous Chapter

In Chapter 17, we explored how entrepreneurs can leverage AI to innovate, scale businesses, and enhance customer experiences. We discussed strategies for AI adoption, tools for operational efficiency, and real-world case studies like Dunzo and Razorpay.

Section 1: The Role of AI in Accessibility

1.1 Empowering Independence

AI technologies enable individuals with disabilities to lead more independent lives by addressing challenges in communication, mobility, and sensory impairments.

- **Example**: AI-powered wheelchairs that assist with navigation.

1.2 Bridging the Digital Divide

AI ensures equitable access to information and digital services, empowering marginalized communities.

- **Example**: Screen readers for visually impaired users to access websites.

Quick Assessment Quiz

1. How does AI empower independence for individuals with disabilities?
2. Name an AI solution that bridges the digital divide.

Section 2: AI-Driven Assistive Technologies

2.1 Vision Assistance

AI enhances accessibility for individuals with visual impairments.

- **Tools and Examples**:
- **Microsoft Seeing AI**: Reads text, describes surroundings, and identifies objects.
- Click Here
- **OrCam MyEye**: Wearable device that converts text into speech.
- Click Here

2.2 Communication Support

AI facilitates better communication for people with hearing or speech disabilities.

- **Examples**:
- **Google Live Transcribe**: Provides real-time transcription of spoken words.
- Click Here
- **Voiceitt**: Translates non-standard speech into understandable language.
- Click Here

2.3 Mobility Enhancements

AI improves mobility and navigation for individuals with physical disabilities.

- **Examples**:
- **Waymo**: Autonomous vehicles that offer transportation solutions.
- Click Here
- **Kinova Robotics**: AI-powered robotic arms for individuals with limited mobility.
- Click Here

Quick Assessment Quiz

1. Which AI tools assist visually impaired individuals?
2. What is the primary function of Google Live Transcribe?
3. How does Waymo improve mobility for disabled users?

Section 3: Inclusive Design Principles

3.1 Designing for All

Inclusive design ensures technology is accessible to people of all abilities.

- **Key Principles**:
- Flexibility in use: Products should accommodate a wide range of preferences and abilities.
- Simple and intuitive: Interfaces should be easy to understand.

3.2 Accessibility Standards

Adhering to international standards like WCAG (Web Content Accessibility Guidelines) ensures inclusivity.

- **Examples**:
- Websites optimized for screen readers.
- Videos with captions and transcripts.

3.3 Collaborative Development

Involving individuals with disabilities in the design process helps create user-centric solutions.

Quick Assessment Quiz

1. What is the significance of inclusive design?
2. Name two principles of inclusive design.
3. Why is collaboration important in developing accessible technologies?

Section 4: Case Studies of AI and Accessibility

4.1 Case Study: Project Euphonia (Google)

AI-powered speech recognition tailored for individuals with speech impairments.

- **Impact**: Enhanced communication and interaction with devices.
- Click Here

4.2 Case Study: SignAll

AI-based software translating sign language into text and speech in real-time.

- **Impact**: Improved communication for the deaf community.
- Click Here

4.3 Case Study: Avaz App (India)

AI-powered communication app designed for individuals with autism and other speech disabilities.

- **Impact**: Facilitated education and personal expression.
- Click Here

Quick Assessment Quiz

1. How does Project Euphonia assist individuals with speech impairments?
2. What is the purpose of the Avaz App?
3. Describe the impact of SignAll on the deaf community.

Section 5: Challenges and Ethical Considerations

5.1 Technological Barriers

AI solutions may not always address the diverse needs of all users.

- **Solution**: Continuous improvement and user feedback loops.

5.2 Cost and Accessibility

High costs can limit access to assistive technologies.

- **Solution**: Develop open-source and low-cost AI tools.

5.3 Privacy Concerns

AI applications often require personal data, raising privacy issues.

- **Solution**: Implement robust data protection measures.

Quick Assessment Quiz

1. What are the main challenges in creating AI for accessibility?
2. How can costs of assistive technologies be reduced?
3. What measures ensure privacy in AI applications?

Chapter Summary

This chapter explored the transformative role of AI in enhancing accessibility. From vision assistance to mobility enhancements, AI-driven tools empower individuals with disabilities. Inclusive design principles and adherence to accessibility standards were emphasized, supported by real-world case studies. Challenges like cost, technological limitations, and privacy concerns were addressed with actionable solutions.

Points to Ponder

1. How can AI further revolutionize accessibility for people with disabilities?
2. What are the key considerations for inclusive design in AI technologies?
3. How can governments and organizations collaborate to make AI solutions more accessible?

Preview of Chapter 19: The Dark Side of AI: Risks and Threats

In **Chapter 19**, we will explore the potential risks and threats posed by AI, including ethical dilemmas, misuse, and the challenges of regulating AI technologies.

References

1. Microsoft Seeing AI - Click Here
2. OrCam MyEye - Click Here
3. Google Live Transcribe - Click Here
4. Waymo - Click Here
5. Kinova Robotics - Click Here
6. Project Euphonia - Click Here
7. SignAll - Click Here
8. Avaz App - Click Here
9. WCAG Standards - Click Here

Chapter Review Quiz

1. Explain the role of AI in bridging the digital divide.
2. Discuss two real-world AI tools for vision assistance.

3. What are the ethical considerations when developing AI for accessibility?
4. How do inclusive design principles contribute to accessibility?
5. Analyze the impact of AI-powered tools like Avaz and SignAll on education and communication.

CHAPTER 19

The Dark Side of AI: Risks and Threats

Learning Objectives

By the end of this chapter, you will:

1. Understand the potential risks and threats posed by AI technologies.
2. Explore ethical challenges in the development and use of AI.
3. Identify cases of AI misuse and their consequences.
4. Learn about regulatory frameworks and the role of governance in mitigating risks.
5. Examine future scenarios and how society can navigate AI's darker implications responsibly.

Recap of Previous Chapter

In Chapter 18, we examined how AI promotes accessibility, empowering individuals with disabilities through assistive technologies and inclusive design. Tools like Seeing AI and Avaz, as well as frameworks like WCAG, were highlighted alongside case studies.

Section 1: Understanding the Risks of AI

1.1 Bias in AI Algorithms

AI systems can perpetuate or amplify existing biases due to biased training data or flawed models.

*   **Example**: Discrimination in AI-driven hiring tools, where algorithms favor certain demographics.

1.2 Privacy Invasion

AI often relies on massive datasets, raising concerns about personal data privacy and misuse.

- **Example**: Facial recognition systems used without consent.

1.3 Job Displacement

Automation and AI threaten jobs in industries like manufacturing, customer service, and transportation.

- **Example**: Autonomous vehicles reducing the need for human drivers.

Quick Assessment Quiz

1. What are the main causes of bias in AI?
2. How can AI systems invade personal privacy?
3. Name one industry significantly affected by job displacement due to AI.

Section 2: Ethical Challenges in AI Development

2.1 Accountability in AI Decisions

AI systems make decisions that may have significant consequences, but accountability often remains unclear.

- **Example**: Autonomous drones making combat decisions.

2.2 Manipulation and Deception

AI-powered tools like deepfakes can be used to spread misinformation or manipulate public opinion.

- **Example**: Deepfake videos used in political campaigns to mislead voters.

2.3 AI Weaponization

The use of AI in autonomous weapons poses a significant global threat.

- **Example**: Lethal autonomous weapons capable of making life-or-death decisions.

Quick Assessment Quiz

1. Why is accountability important in AI decision-making?
2. What are deepfakes, and how can they be harmful?
3. Explain the risks associated with AI weaponization.

Section 3: Cases of AI Misuse

3.1 Cambridge Analytica Scandal

AI-driven data analysis was used to manipulate voter behavior in political campaigns.

- **Impact**: Erosion of trust in democratic processes.

3.2 Facial Recognition Misuse

Widespread use of facial recognition technology by governments for mass surveillance.

- **Impact**: Infringement on privacy and civil liberties.

3.3 Algorithmic Discrimination

AI systems in healthcare misallocating resources due to biased algorithms.

- **Impact**: Inequitable treatment and outcomes for marginalized communities.

Quick Assessment Quiz

1. Describe the role of AI in the Cambridge Analytica scandal.
2. How can facial recognition systems be misused?
3. Provide an example of algorithmic discrimination in AI.

Section 4: Regulatory and Governance Challenges

4.1 The Need for Regulation

Governments and organizations must establish policies to mitigate AI risks.

- **Examples of Frameworks**:
- **EU AI Act**: Aims to regulate high-risk AI applications.
- Click Here
- **IEEE Ethics Certification Program**: Sets standards for ethical AI design.
- Click Here

4.2 Global Collaboration

International cooperation is essential to address cross-border implications of AI misuse.

- **Example**: Partnerships on AI between governments and tech companies.

4.3 Enforcement Challenges

Ensuring compliance with AI regulations requires robust monitoring and enforcement mechanisms.

Quick Assessment Quiz

1. What is the purpose of the EU AI Act?
2. Why is global collaboration important for regulating AI?
3. What are the challenges in enforcing AI regulations?

Section 5: Preparing for AI's Future Risks

5.1 Educating Stakeholders

Awareness and education are critical for developers, users, and policymakers.

5.2 Investing in Ethical AI Research

Promoting research that prioritizes ethical considerations and societal benefits.

5.3 Building Resilience

Developing systems that are robust against misuse while fostering innovation.

Quick Assessment Quiz

1. Why is educating stakeholders important in addressing AI risks?
2. How can investment in ethical AI research mitigate risks?
3. What does building resilience in AI systems involve?

Chapter Summary

This chapter delved into the darker aspects of AI, including risks like bias, privacy invasion, and job displacement. Ethical challenges such as accountability, manipulation, and weaponization were explored, alongside real-world cases of AI misuse. Regulatory frameworks like the EU AI Act and the importance of global collaboration were highlighted. Finally, strategies for preparing for future risks were discussed, emphasizing education, ethical research, and resilience.

Points to Ponder

1. How can biases in AI systems be effectively addressed?
2. What are the ethical implications of autonomous decision-making in AI?
3. What role should governments and private sectors play in regulating AI misuse?

Preview of Chapter 20: The Human-AI Relationship: Finding the Balance

In **Chapter 20**, we will discuss the evolving relationship between humans and AI, exploring how to foster collaboration while maintaining human-centric values in an AI-driven world.

References

1. EU AI Act - Click Here
2. IEEE Ethics Certification Program - Click Here

3. Cambridge Analytica Scandal - Click Here
4. Deepfake Detection Technology - Click Here
5. Algorithmic Accountability in Healthcare - Click Here

Chapter Review Quiz

1. Explain the risks of bias and discrimination in AI systems.
2. What are the consequences of AI misuse in political and surveillance contexts?
3. How do global regulations like the EU AI Act contribute to ethical AI development?
4. Describe strategies for building resilience against future AI risks.

CHAPTER 20

The Human-AI Relationship: Finding the Balance

Learning Objectives

By the end of this chapter, you will:

1. Understand the evolving dynamics between humans and AI systems.
2. Explore strategies for fostering collaboration between humans and AI.
3. Analyze ethical considerations in human-AI relationships.
4. Learn how to maintain human-centric values in an AI-driven world.
5. Reflect on the future of human-AI interaction and the responsibilities of society.

Recap of Previous Chapter

In Chapter 19, we explored the darker side of AI, addressing risks like bias, privacy invasion, and job displacement, along with ethical challenges such as accountability, manipulation, and weaponization. Strategies for mitigating these risks and the importance of global collaboration were emphasized.

Section 1: Understanding the Human-AI Relationship

1.1 Evolution of Human-AI Interaction

From basic automation to conversational AI, the relationship between humans and machines has evolved dramatically.

- **Examples**: Early industrial robots, virtual assistants like Alexa, and autonomous systems in smart cities.

1.2 Co-Existence: Humans and AI

AI systems complement human skills but can also create dependency or ethical dilemmas.

- **Key Consideration**: Balancing AI capabilities with human oversight.

1.3 Trust in AI Systems

Building trust requires transparency, reliability, and ethical use of AI systems.

- **Case Study**: AI-powered diagnostic tools in healthcare that enhance patient outcomes when trusted and used appropriately.

Quick Assessment Quiz

1. Describe how human-AI interaction has evolved over time.
2. What is the role of trust in the human-AI relationship?
3. How can AI complement human skills without fostering dependency?

Section 2: Collaboration Between Humans and AI

2.1 Augmented Intelligence

Rather than replacing humans, AI is increasingly used to augment human decision-making and creativity.

- **Example**: AI tools like Grammarly that improve writing without eliminating human input.

2.2 Hybrid Work Models

In workplaces, AI and humans collaborate to achieve higher productivity and efficiency.

- **Example**: AI scheduling tools paired with human project management.

2.3 Building Synergy

Human intuition and creativity combined with AI's computational power create new possibilities.

- **Example**: AI-assisted drug discovery in pharmaceuticals.

Quick Assessment Quiz

1. What is augmented intelligence, and how does it differ from AI replacing humans?
2. Provide an example of a hybrid work model using AI and human collaboration.
3. How can synergy between humans and AI lead to innovation?

Section 3: Ethical Considerations in Human-AI Relationships

3.1 Autonomy vs. Dependency

Maintaining human autonomy while benefiting from AI's capabilities is a critical balance.

- **Example**: Over-reliance on AI in navigation leading to a decline in human spatial awareness.

3.2 Bias and Discrimination

Ensuring AI systems reflect fairness and inclusivity without perpetuating biases.

- **Example**: Proactive measures in training AI with diverse datasets.

3.3 Privacy and Security

AI systems must respect individual privacy while ensuring secure data handling.

- **Example**: Privacy-preserving AI in personalized marketing.

1. Why is maintaining autonomy important in human-AI relationships?
2. How can training datasets help mitigate bias in AI?
3. Provide an example of privacy-preserving AI.

Section 4: Maintaining Human-Centric Values

4.1 Ethical Design Principles

AI systems should align with human-centric values, prioritizing safety, inclusivity, and fairness.

- **Example**: OpenAI's focus on ethical AI development.

4.2 Empowering Human Agency

Empowering users to control how AI systems operate in their lives.

- **Example**: Adjustable AI settings in social media algorithms for tailored content consumption.

4.3 Promoting AI Literacy

Educating society about AI's potential and limitations fosters responsible usage.

- **Initiative**: India's AI for All program promoting AI awareness among citizens.

Quick Assessment Quiz

1. List three human-centric values AI systems should prioritize.
2. What is AI literacy, and why is it important?
3. Provide an example of an initiative promoting AI literacy.

Section 5: Reflecting on the Future of Human-AI Interaction

5.1 Navigating Ethical Dilemmas

As AI advances, society must navigate complex ethical questions about its role and limitations.

5.2 Preparing for Co-Evolution

Humans and AI will continue to evolve together, requiring adaptability and open-mindedness.

5.3 A Shared Vision for the Future

Creating a collaborative future where humans and AI coexist harmoniously while addressing global challenges.

Quick Assessment Quiz

1. What are some ethical dilemmas society might face with AI's future evolution?
2. How can humans and AI prepare for co-evolution?
3. Describe a shared vision for the future of human-AI collaboration.

Chapter Summary

This chapter explored the human-AI relationship, emphasizing the evolution of interaction, collaboration strategies, and ethical considerations. Maintaining human-centric values and promoting AI literacy are essential for fostering trust and synergy. The future of human-AI interaction requires careful navigation of ethical dilemmas and co-evolution toward a shared vision of progress.

Points to Ponder

1. How can we ensure AI enhances human lives without undermining autonomy?
2. What strategies can build trust and transparency in AI systems?

3. How can society foster a collaborative and ethical future with AI?

Preview of Chapter 1: Introduction to AI: Understanding the Basics

In the next chapter, we begin our journey with a comprehensive introduction to AI, its history, and its transformative role across industries and society.

References

1. OpenAI's Ethical AI Development - Click Here
2. AI for All Program by NITI Aayog - Click Here
3. Augmented Intelligence Overview - Click Here
4. Privacy-Preserving AI Techniques - Click Here
5. Trust in AI Systems - Click Here

Chapter Review Quiz

1. Describe the evolution of the human-AI relationship and its current state.
2. Explain the concept of augmented intelligence with an example.
3. How can human-centric values be incorporated into AI system design?
4. What role does AI literacy play in fostering a responsible future?
5. Outline key challenges in preparing for the future of human-AI interaction.

CHAPTER 21

AI and Government: Transforming Governance and Public Administration

Learning Objectives

By the end of this chapter, readers will be able to:

1. Understand the impact of AI on governance and public administration.
2. Explore how AI enhances policy-making, service delivery, and citizen engagement.
3. Identify challenges and ethical considerations in adopting AI in government.
4. Learn about global examples of AI-powered governance innovations.

Recap of Chapter 20

In the previous chapter, we explored the intricate relationship between humans and AI, emphasizing the importance of ethical, emotional, and strategic approaches to maintaining balance. Building on this, we now turn our attention to how governments worldwide are leveraging AI to revolutionize governance and public administration.

1. The Role of AI in Governance

Enhancing Decision-Making

AI's ability to process large datasets and identify trends makes it an invaluable tool for informed policy-making. Governments use predictive analytics to assess potential outcomes and develop evidence-based strategies.

- Example: Singapore's Smart Nation initiative uses AI to optimize urban planning and resource management.

Automating Routine Tasks

AI streamlines administrative processes, reducing costs and improving efficiency.

- Example: The UK uses AI-powered chatbots to handle routine visa inquiries, reducing workload for immigration officers.

Quick Assessment Quiz:

- Question: What is a key advantage of AI in decision-making for governance?

a) Emotional reasoning

b) Processing large datasets

c) Reducing public engagement

d) Minimizing transparency

2. AI in Public Service Delivery

Improving Citizen Services

AI-powered systems make government services more accessible and efficient. Chatbots, virtual assistants, and automated systems help citizens access information quickly.

- Example: India's UMANG app integrates multiple government services into a single AI-enabled platform for citizen convenience.

Proactive Problem-Solving

AI enables predictive maintenance and proactive service delivery, addressing issues before they escalate.

- Example: In Barcelona, AI monitors urban infrastructure to prevent service disruptions, such as water supply failures.

Quick Assessment Quiz:

- Question: Which of these is an example of AI improving public services?

a) Predictive policing

b) Reactive problem-solving

c) Proactive service delivery

d) Manual data entry

3. AI for Citizen Engagement

Enhancing Transparency and Accountability

AI-powered tools analyze government data, making operations more transparent to the public.

- Example: The US government uses AI in its Open Government Initiative to provide data visualizations that citizens can easily understand.

Encouraging Participatory Governance

AI platforms facilitate two-way communication between citizens and policymakers, enabling more inclusive decision-making.

- Example: Finland uses AI to crowdsource public opinion on national policies.

Quick Assessment Quiz:

- Question: How does AI promote citizen engagement in governance?

a) Reducing access to government data

b) Automating secretive processes

c) Crowdsourcing opinions and enhancing transparency

d) Eliminating public input

4. Challenges and Ethical Considerations

Bias and Fairness

AI systems risk perpetuating biases if not properly managed, potentially leading to unfair policies or discrimination.

- Example: Predictive policing algorithms in the US have faced criticism for disproportionately targeting minority communities.

Data Privacy Concerns

The use of AI in governance involves handling sensitive citizen data, raising privacy concerns.

- Example: The European Union's GDPR includes provisions to ensure ethical use of AI in processing personal data.

Digital Divide

AI adoption can widen the gap between those with and without access to technology, excluding marginalized communities.

Quick Assessment Quiz:

- Question: What is a major ethical challenge in AI governance?

a) Enhancing service accessibility

b) Widening the digital divide

c) Automating unbiased decisions

d) Ensuring privacy compliance

Chapter Summary

AI is transforming governance by improving decision-making, service delivery, and citizen engagement. While it offers immense potential, governments must address ethical challenges like bias, privacy, and inclusivity to ensure fair and effective AI deployment.

Points to Ponder

1. How can governments balance efficiency with ethical AI practices?
2. What strategies can reduce the digital divide in AI-driven public services?
3. How can citizens actively participate in shaping AI policies?

Preview of Chapter 22

In the next chapter, **AI for Small Businesses: Unlocking Growth and Efficiency**, we will explore how small enterprises can leverage AI tools to enhance productivity, reduce costs, and compete in a digital economy.

References

1. "Singapore Smart Nation Initiative" – Smart Nation Singapore
2. "UMANG App by India"

CHAPTER 22

AI for Small Businesses: Unlocking Growth and Efficiency

Learning Objectives

By the end of this chapter, readers will be able to:

1. Understand how AI can help small businesses streamline operations and drive growth.
2. Identify specific AI tools tailored to the needs of small businesses.
3. Explore Indian and global examples of AI adoption in small enterprises.
4. Address challenges small businesses face in implementing AI solutions.

Recap of Chapter 21

In the previous chapter, we explored the transformative role of AI in governance, focusing on its applications in public administration and citizen engagement, particularly in India. We also discussed the challenges of ethical AI deployment in governance. Now, we shift our focus to how small businesses can benefit from AI to grow and compete in today's technology-driven marketplace.

1. How AI Benefits Small Businesses

Streamlining Operations

AI automates routine tasks, reduces manual effort, and enhances operational efficiency for small businesses.

- **Examples:**
- Automating inventory management through AI-powered tools like Zoho Inventory.

- Chatbots like Freshchat handle customer inquiries, allowing businesses to focus on core activities.
- AI systems such as QuickBooks assist in accounting and bookkeeping.

Enhancing Customer Experience

Personalized recommendations and predictive analytics help businesses tailor offerings to individual customer preferences.

- **Examples:**
- E-commerce platforms like Shopify use AI to recommend products based on user behavior.
- Small restaurants in India leverage AI-driven POS systems like Petpooja to analyze customer preferences and design promotions.

Quick Assessment Quiz:

- Question: Which AI tool is commonly used for inventory management by small businesses?

a) QuickBooks

b) Zoho Inventory

c) Canva

d) Freshchat

2. AI Tools Tailored for Small Businesses

Affordable and Accessible Solutions

AI tools are becoming increasingly affordable, making them accessible to small businesses.

Examples:

- Marketing automation tools like HubSpot for lead generation and customer retention.
- AI-based HR tools such as Darwinbox help with recruitment and employee management.

Scalable AI Tools

Small businesses benefit from tools that can scale with their growth.

Examples:

- Google Workspace for automated workflows.
- TallyPrime for financial management, widely used by Indian SMEs.

Quick Assessment Quiz:

- Question: Which tool is widely used by Indian SMEs for financial management?

a) Shopify

b) TallyPrime

c) Canva

d) HubSpot

3. Indian and Global Examples of AI Adoption

Indian Examples

1. **Lenskart** – An eyewear retailer using AI for virtual try-ons and personalized recommendations, enhancing the customer experience.
2. **Zomato** – Uses AI to optimize food delivery routes, ensuring faster service.

Global Examples

1. **Etsy** – Uses AI to match buyers with unique products from small sellers.
2. **Stitch Fix** – Leverages AI for personalized clothing recommendations based on customer preferences.

Quick Assessment Quiz:

- Question: Which Indian company uses AI for optimizing food delivery routes?

a) Flipkart

b) Zomato

c) Swiggy

d) Myntra

4. Challenges in AI Adoption for Small Businesses

Cost Constraints

Many small businesses struggle to afford advanced AI solutions despite their benefits.

- **Solutions:** Exploring free or low-cost AI tools like Google Analytics or ChatGPT.

Lack of Technical Expertise

Small businesses may lack the expertise to implement and manage AI systems.

- **Solutions:** Upskilling staff through online courses or hiring external consultants.

Data Privacy Concerns

Handling sensitive customer data with AI tools raises concerns about privacy and compliance.

- **Solutions:** Adhering to data protection laws like India's Data Protection Bill.

Quick Assessment Quiz:

- Question: What is one way small businesses can adress technical expertise challenges in adopting AI?

a) Ignore AI implementation

b) Upskill staff through online courses

c) Invest only in hardware

d) Focus solely on manual processes

Chapter Summary

AI offers small businesses transformative opportunities to automate processes, enhance customer experiences, and improve efficiency. However, successful AI adoption requires overcoming cost constraints, technical skill gaps, and data privacy concerns. By leveraging accessible and scalable tools, small businesses can unlock their potential in today's competitive landscape.

Points to Ponder

1. What specific AI tools could benefit your small business or a business you know?
2. How can small businesses balance affordability with the need for effective AI solutions?
3. What steps can small businesses take to ensure ethical and responsible AI usage?

Preview of Chapter 23

In the next chapter, **AI in Communication:**

Revolutionizing Media and Social Networks, we will delve into how AI is transforming the way people and organizations communicate, with examples from the media industry and social platforms.

References

1. Google Workspace – https://workspace.google.com
2. TallyPrime – https://tallysolutions.com/tally-prime/
3. Petpooja POS – https://petpooja.com
4. Zoho Inventory – https://zoho.com/inventory
5. Darwinbox HR Solutions – https://darwinbox.com

CHAPTER 23

AI in Communication: Revolutionizing Media and Social Networks

Learning Objectives

By the end of this chapter, readers will be able to:

1. Understand the role of AI in transforming communication channels.
2. Explore the impact of AI on media production, distribution, and consumption.
3. Examine how AI shapes social networks and user interactions.
4. Identify potential challenges and ethical concerns related to AI-driven communication.

Recap of Chapter 22

In the previous chapter, we discussed how AI empowers small businesses by automating processes, enhancing customer experiences, and addressing challenges like cost and technical expertise. We explored tools and examples tailored to small businesses, particularly in India. Now, we delve into how AI is transforming communication, including media and social networks, at a global scale.

1. AI's Role in Communication

Automating Content Creation

AI enables faster and more personalized communication through automated content generation.

Examples:

- AI tools like Jasper and Writesonic generate marketing emails, blog posts, and social media captions.
- In India, companies use AI tools like Pepper Content to create engaging campaigns.

Enhancing Real-Time Communication

AI chatbots and virtual assistants improve customer support and real-time communication.

Examples:

- Platforms like Drift and Intercom provide instant customer query resolutions.

- Indian businesses adopt WhatsApp Business API powered by AI to handle customer interactions seamlessly.

Quick Assessment Quiz:

- Question: Which AI tool is commonly used for generating social media content?

a) Drift

b) Writesonic

c) Intercom

d) WhatsApp Business API

2. AI in Media Production, Distribution, and Consumption

AI in Media Production

AI aids in scriptwriting, video editing, and even generating realistic deepfake videos.

Examples:

- Tools like Synthesia create AI-generated videos for corporate training and marketing.

- Indian media companies like ZEE5 leverage AI for dubbing and content localization.

AI in Media Distribution

AI helps personalize content recommendations based on user behavior.

Examples:

- Netflix's recommendation algorithm curates content for viewers.

- Hotstar in India uses AI to suggest regional content based on user preferences.

AI in Media Consumption

AI powers features like real-time subtitles and adaptive streaming for enhanced user experiences.

Examples:

- YouTube's AI-generated captions assist in accessibility.

- JioCinema's AI-driven adaptive streaming optimizes playback quality based on network conditions.

Quick Assessment Quiz:

- Question: Which Indian streaming platform uses AI for content localization?

a) Netflix

b) ZEE5

c) Amazon Prime

d) JioCinema

3. AI's Role in Shaping Social Networks

Content Moderation

AI identifies harmful or inappropriate content on social platforms.

Examples:

- Facebook and Instagram use AI for filtering hate speech and misinformation.
- Indian platforms like ShareChat leverage AI to moderate regional language content.

Personalized User Experiences

AI algorithms curate social media feeds and suggest connections.

Examples:

- LinkedIn recommends jobs and professional connections based on user data.
- Twitter's AI-driven feed prioritizes relevant tweets for users.

Enhanced Visual Communication

AI tools like Canva and Lumen5 simplify content creation for social media visuals.

Examples:

- Indian startups use Canva to design promotional graphics efficiently.

Quick Assessment Quiz:

- Question: What role does AI play in LinkedIn's operations?

a) Content moderation

b) Job and connection recommendations

c) Visual content creation

d) Adaptive streaming

4. Ethical and Practical Challenges in AI-Driven Communication

Privacy Concerns

AI systems often collect large amounts of user data, raising concerns about privacy.

- **Examples:** Companies must comply with regulations like India's Digital Personal Data Protection Act to ensure data security.

Misinformation and Bias

AI algorithms may inadvertently spread misinformation or exhibit biases.

Examples:

- Instances of biased content recommendations on YouTube.
- The spread of fake news on WhatsApp during elections in India.

Dependence on AI

Overreliance on AI tools can lead to reduced human creativity in communication.

Quick Assessment Quiz:

Question: What is one way to address privacy concerns in AI-driven communication?

a) Collect more user data

b) Reduce AI usage

c) Comply with data protection regulations

d) Ignore privacy issues

Chapter Summary

AI is revolutionizing communication through automation, media production, and social networking. While it brings significant benefits, including personalized experiences and enhanced efficiency, challenges like privacy concerns and misinformation require careful attention. The chapter highlighted Indian and global examples to showcase AI's transformative impact on communication.

Points to Ponder

1. How has AI transformed the way you consume media or interact on social networks?

2. What ethical considerations should be prioritized in AI-driven communication platforms?

3. How can AI tools balance automation with human creativity in communication?

Preview of Chapter 24

In the next chapter, **AI in Security: Safeguarding the Digital World**, we will explore how AI enhances cybersecurity, protects digital assets, and addresses threats like hacking and data breaches.

References

1. Jasper AI – https://www.jasper.ai

2. Pepper Content – https://www.peppercontent.io

3. Synthesia – https://www.synthesia.io

4. ZEE5 AI Dubbing – https://www.zee5.com

5. LinkedIn AI – https://www.linkedin.com

CHAPTER 24

AI in Security: Safeguarding the Digital World

Learning Objectives

By the end of this chapter, readers will be able to:

1. Understand how AI enhances cybersecurity measures.

2. Explore AI's role in identifying and mitigating cyber threats.

3. Examine the ethical implications and challenges of AI in security.

4. Identify future trends in AI-driven security solutions.

Recap of Chapter 23

In the previous chapter, we examined how AI revolutionizes communication through automation, media production, and social networking. Using examples from India and globally, we discussed both the transformative potential and the challenges of AI in shaping modern communication. This chapter shifts focus to a critical area: security, where AI plays a vital role in protecting digital assets and ensuring safety.

1. The Role of AI in Enhancing Cybersecurity

AI for Threat Detection

AI-driven tools analyze vast amounts of data to detect potential threats in real time.

Examples:

- Firewalls integrated with AI, such as Palo Alto Networks' Cortex XDR, proactively detect suspicious activities.

- Indian companies like Quick Heal use AI to identify malware and phishing attacks.

AI for Fraud Prevention

AI systems identify anomalies in financial transactions, reducing fraud in banking and e-commerce.

Examples:

- AI models like those from SAS detect fraudulent credit card activities.

- Paytm in India leverages AI to monitor and prevent transaction fraud.

Quick Assessment Quiz:

Question: Which Indian company uses AI to detect malware?

a) Paytm

b) Quick Heal

c) Palo Alto Networks

d) SAS

2. AI's Role in Mitigating Cyber Threats

Automated Incident Response

AI enables automated responses to threats, reducing response times and mitigating damage.

Examples:

- IBM's QRadar integrates AI to respond to cyber threats instantly.

- In India, Wipro uses AI-driven solutions for cybersecurity incident management.

Securing IoT Devices

With the rise of Internet of Things (IoT) devices, AI protects against vulnerabilities specific to connected devices.

Examples:

- AI platforms like Armis secure IoT ecosystems.
- Indian telecom companies like Jio implement AI for IoT device security in smart homes.

Quick Assessment Quiz:

Question: How does AI contribute to IoT security?

a) By enabling faster internet speeds

b) By detecting vulnerabilities in connected devices

c) By simplifying device installations

d) By replacing physical security measures

3. Ethical Implications and Challenges of AI in Security

Bias in AI Models

AI systems may exhibit biases that lead to false positives or negatives in threat detection.

Examples: AI facial recognition systems have faced criticism for misidentifying individuals based on racial or gender biases.

Privacy Concerns

AI security systems often require large amounts of user data, raising privacy issues.

Examples:

- GDPR and India's Digital Personal Data Protection Act aim to regulate data collection and usage.

- Cases where misuse of surveillance AI has led to privacy infringements.

Dependence on AI

Over-reliance on AI systems can create vulnerabilities if systems fail or are compromised.

Examples: Instances of AI-driven tools being exploited by hackers to bypass security measures.

Quick Assessment Quiz:

Question: What is a major ethical concern related to AI in security?

a) Faster detection

b) Over-reliance on systems

c) Better fraud prevention

d) Increased IoT usage

4. Future Trends in AI-Driven Security Solutions

AI-Powered Predictive Analytics

Future AI tools will predict threats before they occur by analyzing patterns and trends.

Examples: Cybersecurity platforms like Darktrace are pioneering predictive analytics for threat prevention.

Integration of Quantum Computing

Combining AI with quantum computing will enhance encryption and secure communication systems.

Examples: Indian research institutions are exploring AI-quantum integrations for national cybersecurity.

Self-Learning Security Systems

AI systems will evolve to learn from new threats autonomously, reducing dependency on human inputs.

Examples:

OpenAI's advancements in self-learning models could extend to security applications.

Quick Assessment Quiz:

Question: What emerging technology is expected to enhance AI-driven encryption?

a) Blockchain

b) IoT

c) Quantum computing

d) Virtual reality

Chapter Summary

This chapter explored AI's pivotal role in safeguarding the digital world. From threat detection and incident response to securing IoT ecosystems, AI enhances cybersecurity significantly. However, ethical concerns like privacy, bias, and over-reliance require careful consideration. We also discussed future trends such as predictive analytics, quantum computing, and self-learning systems, paving the way for a secure AI-driven future.

Points to Ponder

1. How does AI enhance cybersecurity in your daily digital interactions?

2. What steps should companies take to address ethical challenges in AI-driven security?

3. How can emerging technologies like quantum computing revolutionize AI security systems?

Preview of Chapter 25

In the next chapter, **AI in Sports: Enhancing Performance and Fan Engagement**, we will explore how AI revolutionizes sports analytics, athlete performance, and fan experiences through cutting-edge technologies.

References

1. Quick Heal – https://www.quickheal.com

2. SAS Fraud Detection –

   https://www.sas.com/en_us/solutions/fraud-detection.html

3. IBM QRadar

   – https://www.ibm.com/security/security-intelligence/qradar

4. GDPR Overview – https://gdpr-info.eu

5. Darktrace AI Security – https://www.darktrace.com

CHAPTER 25

AI in Sports: Enhancing Performance and Fan Engagement

Learning Objectives

By the end of this chapter, readers will be able to:

1. Understand how AI revolutionizes sports analytics and performance optimization.

2. Explore AI's applications in improving fan engagement and experiences.

3. Examine ethical concerns and challenges associated with AI in sports.

4. Identify future trends in AI-driven sports innovations.

Recap of Chapter 24

In the previous chapter, we explored how AI strengthens security by enhancing cybersecurity, mitigating threats, and safeguarding IoT devices. The chapter emphasized the importance of ethical considerations and future trends like predictive analytics and quantum computing. This chapter transitions to a lighter yet impactful domain—sports—where AI is transforming both on-field performance and off-field fan engagement.

1. AI in Sports Analytics

Performance Optimization for Athletes

AI-driven tools analyze athlete performance, providing insights into technique improvement, injury prevention, and physical fitness.

Examples:

- Wearable devices like WHOOP track physiological metrics like heart rate variability to optimize training.
- Indian cricket team uses AI analytics to assess player performance and strategize games.

Game Strategy and Decision Making

AI helps coaches and teams make data-driven decisions by analyzing opponents' strengths, weaknesses, and tactics.

Examples:

- AI platforms like Hudl Assist analyze game footage to provide tactical insights.
- Kabaddi teams in India use AI for real-time strategy adjustments.

Quick Assessment Quiz:

Question: Which wearable device helps athletes track physiological metrics?

a) Fitbit

b) WHOOP

c) Apple Watch

d) Garmin

2. AI for Fan Engagement

Personalized Experiences

AI curates personalized fan experiences by analyzing preferences, behavior, and viewing habits.

Examples:

- AI-powered recommendation engines on platforms like Disney+ Hotstar suggest cricket highlights for Indian fans.

- Stadiums use AI-driven chatbots to provide real-time updates and ticketing assistance.

Immersive Technologies

AI enables augmented reality (AR) and virtual reality (VR) experiences, enhancing fan interaction with sports.

Examples:

- Virtual try-outs for fans to "experience" batting like Virat Kohli.

- AI-powered AR tools bring live matches into fans' living rooms.

Quick Assessment Quiz:

- Question: What technology enables fans to interact virtually with sports events?

a) Blockchain

b) Virtual Reality

c) Wearable Devices

d) Machine Learning

3. Ethical and Practical Challenges

Data Privacy Concerns

Collecting and analyzing player and fan data raises privacy issues.

Examples:

- GDPR governs data privacy for AI-driven platforms globally.

- India's Personal Data Protection Bill includes provisions for ethical AI usage.

Overdependence on AI

Reliance on AI tools might reduce human creativity in sports strategies.

Examples: Instances where over-analyzing opponent data led to predictable game plans.

Unfair Advantages

AI tools can create disparities, where teams with higher budgets dominate through advanced technologies.

Examples: Smaller cricket leagues in India often lack access to AI tools available to IPL teams.

Quick Assessment Quiz:

Question: What is a key ethical concern in using AI for fan engagement?

a) Cost of implementation

b) Data privacy issues

c) Overdependence on coaches

d) Low accuracy of analytics

4. Future Trends in AI and Sports

AI-Powered Injury Prevention

Advanced predictive models will foresee potential injuries, helping athletes avoid career setbacks.

Examples:

- AI-integrated smart clothing can detect muscle strain early.
- Research institutions in India explore AI for athlete health monitoring.

Real-Time Broadcasting Enhancements

AI will enable real-time player statistics, multilingual commentary, and personalized match highlights during live streams.

Examples: AI tools providing localized cricket commentary in India.

AI in Esports

As esports grows, AI will enhance player training, audience analytics, and competitive fairness.

Examples:

- Platforms like Dream11 use AI to suggest fantasy cricket team combinations.

Quick Assessment Quiz:

Question: Which future trend focuses on AI for health monitoring in sports?

a) Game Strategy Analytics

b) Smart Clothing

c) AR/VR Engagement

d) Injury Response Systems

Chapter Summary

This chapter highlighted AI's transformative role in sports, from athlete performance optimization to enriching fan experiences. It explored ethical challenges such as data privacy, overdependence, and inequality while providing insights into future trends like AI in injury prevention, real-time broadcasting, and esports.

Points to Ponder

1. How can AI create a balance between technological innovation and human creativity in sports?

2. What measures should be in place to ensure data privacy for players and fans?

3. How can smaller teams leverage AI effectively without huge budgets?

Preview of the Epilogue

The **Epilogue** will weave together the learnings from all chapters, emphasizing AI's profound impact on our lives, while proposing future directions and possibilities for the next wave of AI-driven transformations.

References

1. WHOOP Wearables – https://www.whoop.com

2. Hudl Assist – https://www.hudl.com/products/assist

3. GDPR Overview – https://gdpr-info.eu

4. Disney+ Hotstar AI Features
   – https://www.hotstar.com

5. Dream11 Fantasy Platform
   – https://www.dream11.com

EPILOGUE

Charting the Path Forward

As we conclude *AI and You: A Practical Guide to the Age of Artificial Intelligence*, it's essential to reflect on the journey we've taken together and to connect the threads that weave this narrative into a comprehensive tapestry of understanding, innovation, and responsibility. This epilogue will revisit each chapter's essence, highlight its significance, and look ahead to future possibilities in the AI-driven world.

Chapter Highlights and Their Significance

1. **Introduction to AI: Understanding the Basics**

   This foundational chapter provided a roadmap to AI, exploring its definitions, history, and transformative potential. By setting the stage, it emphasized the need for a balanced perspective on AI's promises and challenges.

2. **AI in Everyday Life: How It's Transforming Our World**

   AI's pervasive influence across daily activities showcased its potential to simplify, enhance, and reimagine tasks, from smart homes to personalized recommendations. This chapter reminded us of the profound changes happening right in front of us.

3. **The Role of AI in the Workplace: Opportunities and Challenges**

   Here, we explored how AI is reshaping industries, enhancing productivity, and creating new job opportunities while also raising concerns about displacement and skill gaps.

4. **AI and Creativity: Partnering with Machines for Innovation**

This chapter demonstrated how AI is not just a tool but a collaborator in creativity, from art to storytelling, inspiring us to rethink the boundaries of human imagination.

5. **Harnessing AI for Personal Growth and Learning**

AI's role in personalized education and self-improvement underscored its potential to empower individuals, foster lifelong learning, and bridge educational divides.

6. **Ethics and Responsibility in AI: Navigating the Challenges**

As the moral compass of the book, this chapter examined the ethical dilemmas and responsibilities of AI developers, users, and policymakers, urging accountability and transparency.

7. **AI and Society: Balancing Progress and Privacy**

Balancing technological advancements with privacy concerns was a recurring theme, emphasizing the need to protect individual rights in a connected world.

8. **The Future of AI: Emerging Trends and Technologies**

This forward-looking chapter outlined emerging AI trends, from quantum computing to explainable AI, urging us to stay adaptable and proactive.

9. **AI for Good: Solving Global Challenges with Technology**

AI's transformative potential for addressing climate change, poverty, and healthcare challenges showcased its role as a force for global good.

10. **Practical Tips for Adapting to an AI-Driven World**
    This chapter provided actionable strategies for individuals and organizations to thrive in an AI-driven era, fostering resilience and adaptability.

11. **AI in Health and Medicine: Revolutionizing Patient Care**

    Highlighting AI's impact on diagnostics, treatment, and research, this chapter emphasized the promise of better healthcare outcomes and ethical considerations in its application.

12. **AI and Education: Shaping the Future of Learning**
    With AI transforming classrooms, this chapter explored how technology can make education accessible, personalized, and engaging for all.

13. **AI in Sustainability: Driving Green Innovations**
    The intersection of AI and sustainability revealed pathways to combat climate change and optimize resource usage, reinforcing the urgency of responsible innovation.

14. **AI in Entertainment: Redefining Creativity and Engagement**
    From personalized streaming to immersive gaming experiences, this chapter celebrated AI's transformative role in entertainment while acknowledging concerns about creativity's authenticity.

15. **AI in Finance: Smart Solutions for Money Management**
    Exploring AI's role in fraud detection, personalized finance, and market predictions, this chapter highlighted its growing influence in reshaping financial landscapes.

16. **AI and Emotional Intelligence: Can Machines Understand Us?**

    The potential of AI to understand and respond to human emotions raised questions about its implications for relationships, trust, and ethical boundaries.

17. **AI for Entrepreneurs: Launching and Growing Businesses with AI**

    Empowering entrepreneurs with AI tools, this chapter celebrated its role in reducing barriers to entry, enhancing efficiency, and scaling innovations.

18. **AI and Accessibility: Empowering Inclusivity**
    AI's capacity to enhance inclusivity for people with disabilities demonstrated its transformative potential to create a more equitable world.

19. **The Dark Side of AI: Risks and Threats**

    By confronting AI's risks, from job displacement to weaponization, this chapter emphasized the need for vigilance, regulation, and collective action.

20. **The Human-AI Relationship: Finding the Balance**
    As a concluding chapter, it reflected on fostering a harmonious relationship between humans and AI, ensuring technology serves humanity's best interests.

Connecting the Dots: An Integrated Perspective

This book is not just a collection of chapters but a narrative that connects the practical, ethical, and philosophical dimensions of AI. Each chapter builds upon the last, weaving a story of AI's profound impact on humanity. From everyday applications to global challenges, from creativity to emotional intelligence, the book underscores the multifaceted nature of AI and its potential to shape our future.

Future Directions

While this book has explored the breadth of AI's current and emerging influence, the journey is far from over. The following areas merit further exploration:

1. **AI and Governance**: Exploring how governments can leverage AI for efficient policy-making while ensuring transparency and equity.

2. **AI and Spirituality**: Investigating the philosophical implications of AI in shaping our understanding of consciousness and the human soul.

3. **AI in Deep Space Exploration**: Examining AI's role in unraveling the mysteries of the universe.

4. **Decentralized AI**: Analyzing the implications of decentralized AI models on privacy, autonomy, and innovation.

Possibilities of a Sequel

A sequel could dive deeper into uncharted territories such as:

- **Post-Singularity Scenarios**: What happens when AI surpasses human intelligence?

- **Global AI Ecosystems**: How nations can collaborate on AI-driven solutions for universal challenges.

- **AI and Human Evolution**: Exploring the interplay between AI and genetic engineering.

- **The Ethics of AI Consciousness**: If machines achieve self-awareness, what responsibilities will humans have?

Closing Remarks

As we close this chapter, we stand on the brink of an extraordinary era, where AI holds the potential to redefine every facet of our existence. But with great power comes great responsibility. The future lies in our hands—not just as passive observers but as active participants, shaping a world where technology serves humanity's highest aspirations.

This book is not an endpoint but a stepping stone. Together, we must continue to learn, adapt, and innovate, ensuring that AI remains a tool for progress, inclusion, and sustainability.

The journey continues—will you join us in writing the next chapter?

Author

Ravindra Dastikop

Book Home: https://dastikop.blogspot.com

LinkedIn: https://LinkedIn.com/in/ravindradastikop